THE
COURT-MARTIAL
OF
CORPORAL
NUTTING

THE
COURT-MARTIAL
OF
CORPORAL
NUTTING

A Memoir of the Vietnam War

JOHN R. NUTTING

Foreword by
Ray M Franklin, Major General, USMC (Ret.)

Skyhorse Publishing

Memoirs are by definition a written depiction of events in a person's life. They are memories. All of the events in this story are as accurate and truthful as possible. Many names have been changed to protect the privacy of others. Mistakes, if any, are caused solely by the passage of time.

Editor's Note

The Court-Martial of Corporal Nutting features selections of trial transcripts and letters written by Nutting when nineteen years old. These have been left unedited and contain the original misspellings and grammar. This serves to illustrate the urgency and lack of resources as experienced by a soldier on the front. There are many mistakes. This is part of the message.

When I first began writing these pages, it was November 15, 2007—forty-one years ago to the day that I arrived in Vietnam. I finally have the courage to tell this story to my children, for them to pass on to their children and beyond before it ceases to exist with my passing.

Foreword

I never met Corporal Nutting in Vietnam, although I am sure at one time or another we were only a few feet apart. He probably sat in the back of my H-53 chopper as we pulled the marines units out of landing zones along the string of outposts—the "McNamara Line"—just south of the DMZ. Con Tien, Gio Linh, and the rock pile were strung out along the line a few miles north of Dong Ha, the last airfield and a piece of near civilization, below the DMZ.

We hauled food, ammo, and medical supplies into the LZs from the Dong Ha LSA (Landing Support Activity) and body bags out to graves registration in Danang.

I was lucky one day when I needed some home services done in my hometown and called Mr. Nutting, who ran his own business, Top Hat Chimney Sweep. We talked several times and got to know one another.

This book is actually two books in one. The combat book is a real page-turner and one of the best I have ever read that truly defines combat action as seen through the eyes of a young marine who lived through the worst of it.

The second book is a sad tale of what it was like stateside waiting to be released from active duty. The military of that time was preoccupied with the War on Drugs.

It seems unbelievable today, forty years later, that we spent so much time and effort trying to convict a combat veteran who had given so much to his country over one marijuana cigarette. We came so close to doing an unbelievable injustice.

The second book is an exposé of our time and should be digested. Somehow, we pushed back from the brink and did not destroy a combat marine's life.

Ray M Franklin, Major General, USMC (Ret.)

1

Almost forty-eight years ago, I stepped into a whole new world. The air was different. It was stifling, heavy—one of those brief periods of sunshine during the monsoon. The red mud was thick and stuck to our stateside boots. Phantom jets rattled our core while we strained to hear some sergeant giving us orders to form up and wait for our gear. Maybe what I remember most from that first day is how a company of marines looked when disembarking from the helicopters.

They were coming back from a mission, and they looked different—different from us. Not because they were grungy and wearing combat gear—it was how they looked if your glance caught their eyes. We were a whole planeload of FNGs,* and they were combat marines who had just gone through some kind of hell. Even though we all were about the same age, they looked in a strange way like they were much older.

Staging in Danang, Vietnam, took a couple of days. We got our shots, received our rifles and web gear—all the things we needed to go into combat.

My new orders came down to proceed to 2nd Battalion, 3rd Marine Division. I climbed into a 4x4 for the trip north. Eight other marines clambered in with me. We rode in the back of the open truck to the Marine's Camp Carroll near the border with North Vietnam. This was the day before Thanksgiving, 1966.

On arrival, I reported to weapons platoon Foxtrot Company, which was about ten miles from Camp Carroll. F Company was stationed around what the marines called "the big tit," a small mountain about one mile south of the demilitarized zone (DMZ). I thought this peak rising above the jungle flatlands looked more like a big tooth jutting out of the jungle than a tit because of its steep sides. Our company occupied bunkers that were somewhat evenly spaced around the entire

---

* Fucking New Guys

circumference at the base of the big tit. In front of the bunkers, facing the jungle was a tangle of concertina wire and claymore mines.

By the time I slogged my way around inside the maze of wire, and finally checked in with my squad, I was really sick, as sick as I could ever remember. I had cramps that would practically double me over, explosive diarrhea, and hot and cold chills. This caused my teeth to rattle.

Once I found my bunker, I crawled up on a sandbag ledge and listened to rats fighting inside the walls. I watched flooding from the torrential monsoon rains cover the bunker floor. I hoped I could fight off the cramps until nightfall. If you had to take a crap during the daylight, some unlucky marine had to go with you through the concertina wire, past the claymore mines, and then stand guard while you dug a quick slit trench and did your business. Nobody wanted to die standing guard over the FNG with the screaming eagle shits. I heard one of the old salts say that although everyone gets the screaming eagles when they first get here, I had it pretty bad.

Corporal Morris Franklin Dixon escorted me—reluctantly—out beyond the wire late in the afternoon, when I could no longer hold back the cramps. I remember Dixon to be an intelligent, thoughtful individual who was married and had a little girl. For some reason he didn't share with anyone at the time he had dropped out of medical school and joined the Marine Corps. Dixon was a kind soul when I needed one.

Several months later I heard he was killed somewhere near Quang Tri.

As we worked our way through the wire back to the bunker, Dixon explained to me that I really did need to hold it until after dark if I could. During the night a marine could work his way up the steep trail, groping his way along in the dark, until he felt the box; then he could have the luxury of a real sit-down—inside the concertina wire. Marines had earlier constructed a very crude toilet: a hole had been cut in a discarded wooden artillery-shell crate and placed over an old foxhole dug on the peak's summit. Dixon pointed to paths behind each bunker disappearing into the brush and winding their ways to the top of the big tit.

Dixon explained that the North Vietnamese Army (NVA) had the "shitter" zeroed in. Intermittently during the night they would fire a shot at it, usually just one. They didn't want us to see their muzzle flash. Dixon said if a marine was able to spot the muzzle flash, the bunkers on that whole side of the hill would open up with rifle and machine gun fire. With a slight smile, Dixon said that it made everyone's day to "call in one hell of a fire mission from the big guns stationed at Con Thien," a small rat-infested firebase a few miles away that had earlier been hacked out of the jungle by the French.

I curled up in my poncho on my sandbag ledge and hoped I could tough out the next few hours, until dark. That night is a blur of vivid nightmares, shivering on the uneven sandbag ledge. I made multiple trips up the steep trail to the shitter that night. The climb at times seemed almost straight up. Red mud on the way had the consistency of thick grease from the relentless, horizontal monsoon rains.

Every marine in the bunker seemed to have different advice on the best route to the top, since the trails intertwined the further up you went. At the top was "the big muddy area." Everyone agreed all I had to do was head for the middle of the muddy area and grope around until I felt the box.

Just before my first trip up the tit, Dixon offered me a smoke. We squatted down in the back of the bunker so the glow of our cigarettes would not be seen. He wanted to give me some last-minute advice and a few words of encouragement. Dixon said that once I found the shitter I needed to blow out as fast as I could and most importantly, lie forward with my chest on my thighs—making myself as small of a target as possible.

It was still dark out on Thanksgiving morning when Dixon woke me up. He told me that if I needed to use the shitter again, I should go now, before it got light. I remember how exhausted I felt by the time I finally reached the top. The sickness and the numerous trips up and down the tit that night had drained away my energy. Also, I felt a different kind of sick feeling in my stomach when I realized that it was starting to get light and there was a whole army out in the early light of dawn who wanted to kill me.

3

I got down into a crouch and moved as fast as I could to the ammo box. As on previous trips, I wiped off the mud around the sitting spot. This time, however, it was light enough that I could see that it wasn't mud I had been wiping away. It was maggots. Millions of maggots! Rippling waves of maggots. The monsoon rain was filling up the foxhole beneath the box, forcing the maggots out. They were all over. Even out in the muddy area. They were in my skivvies, down my pant legs, and in the crack of my butt. I must have added to the collection on every trip. I was so cold and numb and sick, I didn't even feel them. I remember several very long seconds semi-crouching next to the shitter, shaking a handful of maggots out of my pant legs.

The jungle was waking up, and it was almost fully light as I slowly worked my way down the hill. I could feel an NVA soldier behind every rock and bush. By the time I made it back to the bunker I was having serious doubts that I was going to be able to survive thirteen months in this place. I was twenty years old; it was Thanksgiving morning, 1966. I was sick, scared, and homesick. I didn't know my heart could ache like that.

Later in the afternoon for Thanksgiving dinner, I had a can of turkey loaf out of a box of C rations. I remember eating it cold. I didn't feel like lighting a heat tab and warming it up. I then crawled back up on my sandbag ledge and wrapped myself up in a wet poncho. Now it seemed like twice as many rats were fighting near my head as there had been when I left for my "last chance at using the shitter before it got light." I put my fingers in my ears and tried to block out sounds of rats fighting with thoughts of home. I kept thinking, how did I get into this mess?

2

Was it only a year ago I was having Thanksgiving dinner with my family in Sweet, Idaho? Grandma and Grandpa Lock, Uncle Bill and Aunt June, my cousins, and even the family checkers champion, Uncle Ray, was there. My dad carved two turkeys, and my grandmother made my little brother Paul his very own half-sized pumpkin pie.

Was it only a year ago? I was just getting a good start in my senior year in high school. How could I be here, picking maggots out of my butt crack and listening to the rats fight next to my head? How did I get here? I was trapped in a true living nightmare. There was no place to run.

After wallowing in self-pity for a while, my little voice reminded me that I did it to myself; I asked for it. I volunteered for *this*. To enlist I had to sign a medical waiver. I had been in a car wreck my junior year in high school and had chipped a piece off a lumbar vertebrae, and I had inherited my mother's exceptionally flat feet. The thing that concerned the Marine Corps most was that I had a near fatal bout of acute nephritis* when I was thirteen.

I always knew I wanted to be a marine. My dad and his brothers, Dick and Bill, and Uncle Bill's wife, Aunt Mary, all were marines during World War II. Uncle Bill and Aunt Mary's son, Paul, was a marine in Vietnam and had been critically injured with a gunshot wound to the head. Lester Nutting died in battle in World War I. There is a John R. Nutting along with "600 other revolutionary war heroes and several early pastors" interred on top of a hill in Marble Head, Massachusetts. My cousins and I played marines instead of cowboys and Indians. I remember small-town Fourth of July parades, seeing the flags being carried by the old veterans marching by.

My father and Uncle Bill didn't talk much about World War II—not around us kids, anyway. A few times I overheard conversations between my

---

* Kidney failure due to Streptococcus infection

father and Uncle Bill about the price these men and the men they had served with had paid for a word called "freedom." I remember feeling at a young age a sense of pride and a responsibility to my country when I said the Pledge of Allegiance to the flag every morning before school started. That was during America's decade after World War II.

The '50s was not only a decade of healing from the devastation of a world war, but a decade of increasing paranoia. The newspapers, periodicals, and newsreels were filled with patriotic rhetoric. The '50s was a decade of Cold War and an escalating nuclear threat to all. Every child in school knew to "duck and cover" when they heard the town's early warning siren.

My family lived in McCall, Idaho, from 1964 through 1966. My father had taken a job as manager of the Chamber of Commerce. In the mid-'60s McCall was a rustic resort town, built on the edge of Payette Lake. The town's economy depended largely on logging and a flood of summer tourists, plus wealthy flatlanders who owned cabins around the lake. Many of Idaho's "old money" families had fine homes or even large estates here. McCall was so small it didn't have a stoplight, just a blinking amber caution light. When tourists returned home after Labor Day, McCall seemed almost like a ghost town.

In October 1965, during my senior year in high school, my mother gave birth to my little sister Kristine. At that same time, my father and I were having a particularly rough time in our relationship. As long as I could remember my father had been very heavy-handed with his discipline on me, and I was tired of getting knocked around.

Snowfall during the winter of 1965–66 was unusually heavy. By January, the snow finally slid off our metal roof, blocking our windows up to the gutters. The outline of my 1961 Ford, with its special Hearst Mystery shifter, had long disappeared under the growing mountain of snow next to the driveway.

It was during that time that my father and I had an argument, where he hit me hard several times. This ugly incident happened in the back area of his Chamber of Commerce office. I told him then that I was going to quit high school and join the Marines just to get away from him. He told me, in retaliation, that I would not make the sweat on a marine's nuts and that I would be lucky if the navy would take me.

I knew right then that nothing was going to stop me from being a marine. Now, as I think back about that time, it seems appropriate to share a story that happened as a result of this fight with my father.

After our big blowout, my father banished me to my room every night after school. One night, several nights into my punishment, I stepped out my second-story bedroom window, onto the snowdrift from the roof, and trudged off in a heavy snowstorm to the Doghouse.

The Doghouse was the only restaurant/tavern open for miles around. I think the Doghouse saved my sanity during that time. Most of the time through the long winter there was absolutely nothing to do after school. The local radio station played country music from 6 a.m. to 6 p.m., and we didn't have television reception. The Doghouse was the only place during the winter after dark where you could meet your friends, drink coffee, eat greasy cheeseburgers, smoke cigarettes, and play hundreds of games of Spokane roulette.*

No one was in the restaurant area of the Doghouse when I ordered my cheeseburger and coffee. I was half-finished when Bill Acker, McCall's police chief, came stomping in through the front door of the Doghouse, covered with snow and mad as hell. I had always wondered what my dad had on Bill Acker or what kind of strings he pulled. When my dad had checked my room to see if I was still studying and found the room empty, he phoned Chief Acker and told him to arrest me and put me in jail for the weekend. Chief Acker probably wouldn't have been so pissed off about putting me in jail, except that McCall's jail at that time was unusable; it

---

* Spokane roulette: Start with a water glass partially filled with water and stretch a napkin over the opening secured with a rubber band. Place a penny in the center of the napkin. Using a burning cigarette (remember it's 1965 and still cool to smoke) burn a hole anywhere on the napkin, flicking its ash into the water. Each participant takes turns until the penny is supported by the napkin's fine little ribbon-like threads. The player who makes the burn that drops the penny into the water must drink the glass's contents.

was a tiny cinderblock affair built at the turn of the century and was used only to house drunken tourists in the summertime.

I don't think Police Chief Acker said a dozen words to me as he drove the thirty miles to Valley County's jail in Cascade, Idaho. It was near whiteout conditions, and we both strained to see the road through the huge snowflakes as the police car cut fresh tracks in the snow. When Chief Acker locked me into the main cell area, he told me to grab a bunk and make myself comfortable for the night. He said he would talk to my dad, and I would probably be out of there by the next afternoon. He added that the single other inmate, Bob, would cook me up something if I was hungry. Past an area of individual cells was a kitchen area in the back. After Chief Acker left, Bob waved me back into the kitchen. Walking past the cells I noticed several large stacks of men's magazines in one. I remember thinking this may turn out okay after all.

I started working my way through the first stack of magazines as Bob made me bacon, eggs, and toast and filled me in on the details—at least the ones he could remember—on why he was in jail. For years Bob and his best friend, who was a Basque shepherd, would get together after the shepherd had brought his herd out of the high country for the winter. They would buy several cases of whiskey, go out to Bob's house on the lake, and drink for weeks, sometimes a month or better. Bob couldn't remember how long they had been on this bender, only that they had drunk "a shitload" of whiskey. Bob woke up one morning to find his friend with a knife sticking out of his chest. He didn't remember any of it. He couldn't believe he'd done such a thing. He seemed devastated.

That night when I was reading my way through the second stack of men's magazines, I heard coming from one of the back cells Bob making muffled sobbing sounds.

The winter months crawled by, as it never seemed to stop snowing. During the ski season that winter, I had a job at Brundage Mountain on the weekends when the ski hill was open. Many weekends during the ski season, Peg's Teen Inn opened up. Having a place to dance and socialize was a bright spot in the winter doldrums for many of the local teens with cabin fever. Peg made a fortune through the summer months, bringing fledgling rock n' roll bands up from Boise. Her "bubba" husband Frank cooked the burgers and hot dogs and acted as a bouncer when a drunk needed to be thrown out. I know he liked that part the best, especially if it was one of those "snotty-nosed rich kids." The irony is that it was Frank and Peg's oldest daughter who bought alcohol for us local boys, especially if we wanted the "real good stuff" from the state liquor store, like lime or cherry vodka or sloe gin.

In a small-town high school, nothing that has any gossip value at all stays quiet for long. And about the time spring cross-country track season started, most of the "usual suspects" had been grilled by the high school principal about reports of excessive alcohol consumption. I am not quite sure how it came about—probably between the principal and the school board—but the decision came down that eight of us on the track team could warm-up by running down to the Episcopal Church for some "evils of alcohol" counseling on how to improve the quality of our askew lives.

The Reverend Stanton Tate was the closest thing McCall Idaho had for a counselor at that time. In his early to mid-thirties, the Reverend Tate was a kind, insightful man who I liked immediately and soon respected highly—partly for his olfactory fortitude, as all of us were just starting to break a "real good" sweat when we packed into his not-so-spacious office for our rap sessions.

At our final rap/counseling session, Reverend Tate informed us a decision had been made that it would be a great opportunity for us to pay back any wrong we had brought upon the community by cleaning up the old cemetery of the litter and branches that had accumulated over the winter. Most of us showed up that following Saturday. I remember it was a beautiful spring day, with a bright blue sky and an occasional puffy white cloud. The air was still quite chilly, with crusty patches of snow in the shaded areas.

For the first couple of hours, my classmates and I made a large dent in the work we had to do, if only just to keep moving and stay warm. At some point in the early afternoon, after we had worked our way around to the backside of the cemetery and were taking a smoke break in the bright sun, two cases of beer were brought to us by Roy Fleetwood. Roy was one of those polite, easygoing small-town boys, and he had a big crush on my sister Vikki. He was killed in a car wreck while I was Vietnam. It seems our "anonymous benefactor"—Peg and Frank's really hot, but way "too mature" for us, daughter—greatly appreciated the fact that none of us had ratted her out.

I have a bittersweet memory of that afternoon of six or eight guys, backs up against old tombstones, laughing, smoking, and drinking beer in the cool spring sunshine. A few days later, I graduated from high school along with my forty-three classmates.

(Thirty-five years later I returned to that cemetery to find so many of the people who were part of my life at that time, including a number of high school friends, were now buried there.)

My waivers had been accepted, and I was free to join the Marine Corps. The Marine Corps recruiter patiently waited in the audience while I participated in my last stage performance as the Count Mount Joy in McCall-Donnelly High School's 1966 presentation of *The Mouse That Roared*. I had barely wiped the makeup off and received a few hugs and handshakes before the recruiter whisked me off to Boise to be sworn into the Marine Corps.

3

The fact that I was heading to Marine Corps boot camp, and more than likely on to Vietnam, hardly entered into my awareness. I was flying on a jet plane. I had always dreamed of flying ever since I saw crop dusters diving down to the fields in southern Idaho. This certainly wasn't crop dusting, but I had a window seat, and the feeling was more wonderful than I had imagined. I rarely peeled my face from the window the entire flight. All too soon this exciting experience ended when the plane touched down in San Diego. I couldn't believe it; here I was in Southern California, home of the Beach Boys, surfers, and real California girls.

Making my way through the airport to my designated gate for the transfer, seeing all the people, all the hustle and bustle, made me feel a little giddy. I felt like smiling for no other reason than life felt so damn good at that moment.

Locating the designated gate area, I joined a group of other guys about my age, all with the same orders. Soon, we boarded a bus for the short ride to the Marine Corps Recruit Depot. The moment the bus came to a halt in the parking lot, the door flew open and in stormed a wild-eyed staff sergeant drill instructor. He made it crystal clear—at the top of his lungs that our lives as "slimy pieces of civilian shit" had now ceased to exist. The angry face that, as the sergeant paced the length of the bus, further informed us—in various tones that made my chest constrict—we were now an even lower form of life: a Marine Corps recruit. And "as walking amoebas," we needed to "get our sorry asses off the bus, in an orderly fashion, put our feet on the yellow footprints painted on the parking lot surface, put our thumbs along the seams of our trousers, and lock our squirrely eyeballs straight ahead."

I had an advantage over a lot of those guys. I had been well briefed by friends and family who had been in boot camp before. I was in excellent shape from training for track season in the high Idaho Mountains. It was easy for me to tune out loud tirades after living with my father. I knew it was the drill instructor's job to weed out all the flakes and sandbaggers. No matter what I felt on the inside, I was very serious on the outside. I was going to be the very best marine I possibly could be, no matter what.

My experience in Marine Corps boot camp was similar in most respects to any other Marine Corps recruits. There were, however, several events in boot camp that were very memorable. I was assigned to Platoon 1026, known as the "wetback" platoon, because many of the recruits and drill instructors were Mexican-Americans. Our drill instructors, Gunnery Sergeant Padilla and Staff Sergeants Garcia and Hatton, took no time at all in convincing us during our initial introduction that they were "hair-trigger psychopaths" who could go off at nothing more than just eye contact.

About three weeks into boot camp—about the time it takes the drill instructors to completely pulverize any ego that a recruit has left—I was called out of morning formation. I remember my heart sinking clear into my boots, because the last thing you want is to be singled out for *anything*. The word came down that I was to report to a certain Quonset hut over in "headquarters area." About six weeks before I went into boot camp, my father had taken a job managing the Chamber of Commerce in Elko, Nevada. My mother and my siblings moved to Elko later after school was out in McCall. There was some confusion at headquarters about my home address and they wanted me to clear it up.

I know my ass was puckered up to a ten plus, standing at attention in front of the entire platoon. I had no trouble hearing Sergeant Padilla as he gave me directions on how to get to headquarters—with his face about an inch from my nose. He ended his instructions with "now double-time your sorry ass down there, private, and square this fuck up away." It seemed like I double-timed forever through a maze of Quonset huts until I found the right one. I knocked loudly three times on the door, and a voice yelled "enter." I strode briskly over to the large desk, snapped my heels together, dug my thumbs along the seams of my trousers, locked my squirrely eyeballs straight ahead, and reported loudly, "Sir, Private Nutting reporting as ordered, *sir*." I had barely gotten the last "sir" out of my mouth when the female sergeant behind the desk sprang to her feet, leaned way over her desk and up into my face, and yelled, "You dumb shit, do I look like I have a set of nuts hanging between my legs? It's 'ma'am,' you dumb shit, *ma'am*."

About that time I might've looked like a marine on the outside but the whole ordeal just about folded me up on the inside. Long before all the information was squared away and she cut me loose, I had gained a new appreciation for the term "sweating bullets." I heard a stifled snicker from one of the woman marine clerks in the room as I stepped outside the Quonset hut. I put on my cover (hat) and stepped up my double-time pace to a full-on run back to the relative safety of Platoon 1025.

Amazingly, even under these circumstances, I found myself in a strange way enjoying boot camp. I was highly motivated, and I found what I was being taught not only challenging but very exciting. I soon discovered that anything physical was far easier here at sea level in San Diego than my accustomed mountains of Idaho. Consequently, I could compete with the top guys in my platoon. The first black person I remember knowing person-ally, and a marine who I liked right off the bat, was a recruit named Clifford Guinn.

June 27, 1966

Dear Mom and Dad,
Guess what?
Our platoon had this big contest on the obstacle course. This big Negro guy and I had left the whole platoon behind, and were on the last section of the run. I started to pull ahead of him, when I got on a balance log, lost my balance, and fell off. I'm in the hospital. I just sprained my ankle—the same one I always do. So I'm laid up for a little while. Since our platoon is on mess duty, I won't miss anything. Boy, this is the shits. I am getting real tired of listening to a bunch of hypochondriacs thinking of ways to get out of the Corps. Today is Saturday, and I'm still in the hospital. I guess I turned my ankle worse than I thought, I can only hope to get out by Monday. My platoon commander must like me in a sadistic sort of way. He said he was going to keep me in his platoon, just to work my ass off. You see, if you miss three days

of training they drop you, and I have missed four already, so I consider myself pretty lucky. This is some place. They've got a queer locked up, not 10 feet from me, and of course the chicken shit is thinking of a way to get himself discharged. One guy cut his index finger off, all sorts of guys like that. All I have to say about this place is more power to them; I wouldn't want them in a foxhole with me.

Love,
John

Immediately after I left the hospital, our "series"* came off mess duty. The next thing for us was our first drill competition on the main parade deck. Our "series" consisted of Platoons 1025–1028, the marine recruits with whom we competed in every aspect of our training. I remember feeling a little extra nervous about the first drill competition. I had been selected as the marine who marched in front of the platoon, carrying the red and gold pennant with our platoon number, 1025, sewn on it. Platoon 1025 was the first platoon on the drill field. And I was first stepping on the parade ground. We ended up doing surprisingly well, with the exception of Private Gomez, who fell out of step a couple of times.

We in Platoon 1025 were standing at parade rest on the edge of the parade deck when Platoon 1026 marched by. The marine recruit who carried pennant for Platoon 1026 was a tall skinny redheaded marine who reminded me of a stork. His name was Harold Banta Robinson. Just as Platoon 1026 marched by us, the drill instructor ordered a left flank, and the entire platoon executed a smart left-flank move—except for Robinson. Somehow, Robinson didn't hear the order and kept marching straight ahead—alone. The sight of him marching off by himself was more than I could hold in. I'm not sure I laughed out loud, but my drill instructor caught me grinning, and that was enough!

After the drill competition was over and we were still in formation, Robinson and I were ordered from the ranks and to double-time over to the sand pits. There we were instructed to do squat thrusts "for-fucking-ever."

---

* Series is a term for platoon

It took about fifteen minutes shout-counting out squat thrusts before our junior drill instructor, Garcia, grew bored of haranguing us. He threatened us with unimaginable grief and misery if we even as much as thought about stopping. He then went to the drill instructors' Quonset hut in search of a cup of coffee.

Robinson and I got acquainted under these strange circumstances. He was an avid music fan and had a big record collection of all the top groups. I didn't tell him that the last record I had bought was a 45 rpm of the Beatles' "I Want to Hold Your Hand." Somewhere in that conversation, Robinson asked me if I had ever smoked pot—maybe he said marijuana. I said no, but I knew a little about it. I spent some time with a couple of summer girls from Salt Lake City who told me about the two or three times they had tried it. Robinson told me he was from Corpus Christi, Texas, where his dad was a physician with a family practice. I don't think I believed him at the time, but Robinson said his dad told him that the best thing for him to do was to stay away from all drugs and alcohol. But if he was going to experiment with anything, his dad would rather see him use marijuana. His dad also said that he felt marijuana would be far safer than drinking tequila, and he would be less likely to do anything really stupid. That's the last time I spoke with "Robbie" until after our series came back from the rifle range.

The pressure on the recruits increased about a hundred fold when the series was bused to Camp Pendleton rifle range for rifle qualification week. At our initiation lecture—not to put any additional pressure on us—one drill instructor sarcastically pointed out "a marine that fails to qualify with his rifle is not a marine and is a lower form of life than a sailor." The pressure was on everybody. You could feel it. The pressure was on the drill instructors too; it reflected badly on them if they turned out a "non-qual." We broke our rifles down and put them back together—blindfolded. We slept with our rifles, and we sang to our rifles, "This is my rifle [holding the rifle in one hand]. This is my gun [grabbing your crotch with the other hand]. This one's for fighting, and this one's for fun." If our platoon was not on the range practicing, we were busy developing the "spit shine and polish" image of a marine. Life when not on the range included heavy physical training and at least one big inspection a day. Random rifle, foot locker, and personal gear inspections could happen at any time, and the squad-bay always had to be in impeccable condition.

Like every other marine on qualification day, I woke up that morning with my stomach in a knot and feeling like I was having some kind of panic attack. We all heard the horror stories of what happens to a recruit who is a "non-qual," especially during the forced march after qualifications.

I had gone over in my head so many times the techniques I would need to qualify with the M-14 rifle. This was the Marine Corps' battle rifle. A reliable selective fire automatic rifle, when on automatic it would fire 700–750 rounds per minute. The M-14 used 7.62 mm NATO ammunition with an effective range of around five hundred yards. I spent many hours just getting into prone, sitting, and standing positions, while running the recruits mantra "BRASS"—Breathe, Relax, Aim, Slack, and Squeeze—in my head. Now it was "either you is, or you ain't" time. I had gone through every step at least a million times in the last week, either on the range or in dry fire visualization.

And now here I was on the line, chambering a live round. I couldn't believe how smoothly it went. Every position felt so natural, and maybe for the first time the M-14 felt like an extension of my body. Our drill instructors called our platoon to attention after the last man came from the firing line. As they called out a marine's name and his score, I felt confident that I had at least qualified—I knew I had hit more bull's-eyes than I ever did before in practice.

It's hard to explain how I felt inside while marching back to the barracks after I qualified on the rifle range. I had shot expert. I had done it! I felt different. I felt a new sense of confidence and pride within myself. At the barracks, we were ordered to fall out, put on full field gear, and form back up in front of the barracks for the dreaded forced march "ASAP."

I was still in the squad bay, filling my canteen, when I heard a muffled shot. A recruit in the barracks on the second floor had failed to qualify; he'd taken a round* off the rifle range and had shot himself in the head. We

---

* Bullet

all had to evacuate the squad-bay and stand in formation outside until the ambulance took his body away.

I don't remember quite how long our forced march was, but I remember it was brutal. The trudging along the hot, dry, well-worn paths seemed to go on forever. This was in mid-July, in full combat gear, humping the thick, dust-covered trails in the back hills of Camp Pendleton. The forced march was a demanding challenge for the marines who qualified on the rifle range. It was an absolute nightmare for the marines who didn't qualify. Along the entire march the non-quals were made to do things such as run recon missions to the top of nearby hills, or they were made to lie prone in the flour-like dust along the side of the trail, dust that seemed to be at least half a foot deep. I felt really bad for those guys. Troops had to double-time past them, with a rhythmic stomping cadence, and any marine who didn't seem to be kicking up enough dust would be invited to join them.

We had about two weeks remaining in boot camp when the buses brought us back from the rifle range to the Marine Corps Recruit Depot (MCRD) in San Diego. On the bus ride back, I realized that unless some catastrophe befell me I was going to make it through Marine Corps boot camp. Spraining my ankle, however, had me very worried about graduating with my platoon. And like all recruits I had lost sleep worrying about qualifying with my M-14. But now that was behind me.

Graduation day at the MCRD began with a white glove inspection from our drill instructors, who looked for any overlooked molecule of dust in a rifle bore or an errant "Irish pennant" on a uniform. What a feeling I, and the former "worthless amoebas" around me, had as we passed the drill instructors' inspections with flying colors. Our chests were filled with personal satisfaction as our heels hit the parade deck in perfect unison. The grand finale of graduation day was the final drill competition on the main parade deck, followed by a few awards and speeches, and then the base commander officially welcomed us into the Marine Corps. Within the hour, we were loaded onto buses and taken to Camp Pendleton for advanced infantry training.

Infantry training taught us how to be at least familiar with the weapons in the Marine Corps arsenal. We threw grenades, fired machine guns, shot the "0351" bazooka, calibrated and fired the mortar, and one particularly memorable experience involved the use of the gas mask.

We were all marched into a building with our gas masks on, and then a drill instructor popped a tear gas grenade. We then were instructed to remove our gas masks and sing the "Marine Corps Hymn" at the top of our lungs. Only then, could we put our gas masks back on, clear them, and march out in an orderly fashion. Well, that's what they told us we were to do, anyway. Almost immediately, snot was flying and recruits were all over the floor crawling, slobbering, their bloodshot eyes gushing tears. Some panicked and tried to force the door open. It seemed like forever before the instructors were satisfied with our rendition of the "Marines Corps Hymn" and allowed us to put our gas masks back on and clear the tear gas out of them. One of the DIs kicked the bolt holding the door closed, and the most beautiful beam of sunlight lit up our almost pitch black Quonset hut coffin. For the next ten minutes or so, there were about fifty young marines crawling around in the dry, sunburned grass of Camp Pendleton, pouring out tears and snot.

In between the classes on armament and fire team tactics, we had daily inspections. Almost every night we ran patrols, practicing setting up ambushes or listening posts. More than once during that time I shared a foxhole with my old boot camp friend Harold Robinson. During the long nights of waiting for our "enemy" to attack us, we actually had enjoyable conversations. I felt I could learn quite a bit from a guy who could talk for an hour about some obscure blues artist or about the "bitchin'" new top hit. It seemed like no matter what we started out talking about, I would end up asking him questions about marijuana. I found my curiosity growing.

In mid-September 1966, I graduated from second infantry training regiment to a basic infantry specialty school, where I learned how to be a "0351 man." A 0351 man? An antitank assault man? What the hell? How did I get picked for that? I didn't think the Viet Cong even had tanks.

September 16, 1966

Dear Mom and Dad,

I was talking to our First Sergeant yesterday, and ask them how they chose who does what. And he said, "They just take platoons in boot camp. The word comes down that they need 400 cooks or 1000 infantrymen and they just take the whole series in that group." This is the case for me. He said that in the time of war, they didn't look at your scores on your test or your school record, or care how much schooling you had. He said I could go to recon school after leave, and I told them I'd think on it. It's a pretty hairy job. He told me he would put me in for meritorious PFC. I should get it after leave. It made me feel pretty good. It means I don't have to wait six or eight months, like everyone out of 256. There were three of us in all. This week, we will march in the LA parade. Audie Murphy, Medal of Honor winner and most decorated soldier of World War II, General Doolittle and others will be there. It's quite a big deal. It will be televised on all the stations around here. This week we will also be riding in helicopters. I guess the pilots need practice.

Love,
John

During the following weeks my training concentrated on learning how to fire the 0351 antitank assault weapon,* and qualifying with the .45 caliber pistol—my side arm. I also learned about making shape charges with plastic explosives for blowing bridges and bunkers, and shooting the "L.A.W.," a small lightweight rocket with a disposable fiberglass launch tube. All other time was spent in seemingly endless physical training sessions, inspections, rifle drills, and practicing fire team tactics in the foothills of Camp Pendleton.

As luck would have it, on the last overnighter in the field before we graduated and headed home for our much-anticipated twenty days of boot leave, I spent part of the night in a foxhole with Harold Robinson and his boot camp buddy named Powers. Our orders had been posted

---

* The bazooka

after morning formation that day. Most of us in our series, we three included, had received orders for Vietnam. When the conversation got around to marijuana, we all agreed that it would be a good idea if Robbie would bring some back after boot leave so Powers and I could try it. After all, we were going to Vietnam, and at that time the war seemed to be escalating weekly—judging by the number of marines coming home in boxes. Trying pot for the first time seemed like a very low-risk adventure considering where we were headed.

4

My orders were to take twenty days leave, after which I was to report back to Camp Pendleton to a staging battalion, with Westpac orders to Vietnam.

Going home on leave to visit my family in Elko, Nevada, was the first time I wore my Marine Corps dress uniform out into the civilian population. I noticed that I saw myself in a different way and that people were making eye contact with me, or even nodding and smiling. I was only a private in the Marine Corps, with a National Defense Ribbon and an Expert Rifleman Medal on my chest, but I was very proud of what I represented.

Although it only had been four months since I'd left for boot camp, it did seem almost like another lifetime. My siblings seemed more grown up, and my parents treated me differently. I could do no wrong in my mother's eyes, and she made cookies and special meals for me. I slept in late and got about a thousand hugs every day. Even though she tried to hide it, sometimes in her face I could see how afraid she was for me. It was awkward for my father and me to relate to each other as adults at first; however, our relationship improved greatly in the days that followed.

My family had rented an old farmhouse on a huge—something like 150,000 acres, ranch about fifteen miles out of Elko, Nevada. The ranch was located on a high desert plateau next to the Ruby Mountains. Being so isolated, and since I didn't know anybody, I spent many hours riding my sister's horse, Lady. We just plodded along, with the family dog, Popo, trotting alongside, sniffing for her nemesis, the jackrabbit. Riding in the quiet serenity of the high desert gave me much-needed time to collect my thoughts. The last four months had been so full; I hadn't really had time to look at the bigger picture. I was a nineteen-year-old faced with the fact that I was going to war with a "grunt" M.O.S. (military occupation specialty). The undeniable reality of my situation was clear: there was a very good possibility I might have to kill someone, or I might not live long enough to get to vote.

One afternoon toward the end of my leave, I saddled up Lady and strapped my dad's .410 bore shotgun to the saddle. Popo and I went hunting for a jackrabbit. We had been out for about an hour when Popo flushed one out in front of me, on the left. I drew a long bead as the rabbit ran in a wide half-circle to my right and fired. The shot hit the rabbit in the hind-quarters, just knocking it down. Then it started to scream. The jackrabbit's scream sounded almost like a little kid screaming. This gave me a cold, sick, guilty feeling in the pit of my stomach when I had to shoot it again to kill it.

On my way back to the farmhouse I remember having serious reservations about myself and about my situation. If I had that much trouble shooting a jackrabbit, then I was in trouble. I prayed very hard going back to the house that day, just asking God to help me out here. There was no way I was going to run. I didn't want to be the reason why some marine got killed—or even myself getting killed because I didn't react in time. I prayed out loud that if God were truly out there, like my grandfather Lock always said he was, then maybe he would help me out. All I knew was, in my heart of hearts, that no matter what, when the time came, I would be on that plane and I would go.

* * * *

A couple of days before I was to head back to San Diego, my dad had a Chamber of Commerce meeting in town. He told me to put on my uniform and that after his meeting he would take Mom and me to check out the casinos and paint the town a little. He dropped us off at the Stockmen's Casino and Hotel and went to his meeting. (I told this story a few times in Vietnam when I or anyone else needed a little cheering up.)

Even in my Marine Corps uniform, I had such a young face that I was immediately asked for identification. After checking the numbers on my driver's license, a sympathetic doorman with a huge beer gut said with a reluctant shrug, "I'm real sorry, Marine, but ya can't be in the bar or gamble."

It was no big deal. I wasn't interested in drinking, and I didn't have any money to gamble. Mom and I went over to the coffee shop and had a great talk while we waited for Father. When Father showed up and found out that we had been refused entry to the casino area, it just lit his fuse. He was saying something like, "If my boy is old enough to go and fight in Vietnam, then he is old enough to drink a beer or put a quarter in a slot machine in this two-bit, cracker-ass casino!" His voice faded away into the sounds of multiple slot machines as he stormed off, looking for someone's ass to chew.

A few minutes later my father came back with two official-looking guys—I think one was the head pit boss. We were given a lot of extra special treatment after that, including front row center seats to their floor show. It was called the Las Vegas Follies Revue. The show was a kind of raunchy, burlesque strip show. The showgirls were down to their tasseled nipple pasties and their fringed G-strings when I was called up on stage for a bogus "men in uniform" interview.

The mistress of ceremonies and star of the Follies Revue was an older performer with extra-large breasts, platinum blond hair, and the gravelly voice of the heavy smoker. With her cigarette breath close to my face, she asked me a series of dumb sexual innuendo questions while my parents were less than ten feet away. The Las Vegas Follies Revue "men in uniform interview" finale was me sitting on a stool while they did a star-spangled salute to the armed forces. The big-breasted star marched past me more than a few times bouncing her huge tits within inches of my face in time to the music.

In the coming months I would think about that scene many times when I was on watch or just feeling lonesome. Somehow that whole scenario never failed to make me smile.

The following day I took Lady out for the last time—without the shotgun. When I returned, my father was waiting at the corral gate. I told my father about the incident with the jackrabbit, and the self-doubt I was having about being a combat marine. It's not so much his words I remember, but the look on my father's face. It was all out of his control. His son was going to Vietnam as a Marine Corps grunt, and there was nothing he could do about it. He told me he loved me and that he was proud of me. I gave my father a hug. We were just two human beings who loved each other, and we hadn't shared that very much in our lives.

My dress green uniform was impeccable when I boarded the old twin-engine DC 3. I felt proud of my uniform and proud that I had earned the privilege to wear it. I had spent most of the evening before packing my gear, shining my brass, and spit shining my shoes. It was tough saying good-bye to my family at the Elko Airport. I kept swallowing a big lump in my throat as I found my seat on the right side of the plane.

What happened next I thought about many times during the next year. By the time the plane was loaded up and taxied to the end of the runway, my feelings returned to near-normal. The plane's engines roared, straining to pick up speed, and I closed my eyes and thought, *Okay, here we go.* As the plane lifted off, I opened my eyes and looked out the window. I saw my dad's funky-blue tuna boat of a car. His Pontiac Bonneville was pulled over on a one-lane road that ran parallel to the runway. My family was all standing out in the road, waving good-bye at my airplane.

There I was, nineteen years old, realizing that this might be the last time I would ever see my family. It struck a deep emotional chord. This was the turning point. I was in a small airplane, and everyone knew there was a marine on board. I could not let myself feel what was welling up inside of me or I would embarrass myself and the Marine Corps. Before the Pontiac faded from view, I knew a change had happened within. No, I wasn't going to lose it. Sure, it hurt, but I was a marine, a Marine Corps grunt, and I was going to Southeast Asia to help some "Vietnamese folks" fight Communism. I settled back in my seat with that heady kind of whatever-happens-next-it's-out-of-my-control feeling as the plane gained altitude over the high desert with the Ruby Mountains disappearing behind on its way to Camp Pendleton, California.

5

Staging battalion was comprised of a conglomerate of marines from every echelon of the Marine Corps. All marines who had received orders for Southeast Asia were put together in a temporary staging battalion. Officers, enlisted lifers, and greenhorns like me just out of boot camp; every MOS needed to fill out an infantry battalion was included.

Those of us in the staging process endured three weeks of classes, needed extra shots for Southeast Asia, and inspections. But mostly we were engaged in war games in the hills of Camp Pendleton. For some of us nineteen-year-old, hard-as-nails boot marines, it was the same old thing we had been doing for the last four months, so most of it was a breeze. Watching the old lifers, who had grown soft over the years, getting their asses kicked while humping a full pack on a long exercise boosted our young egos.

A couple of days into staging, I met up with Robinson and Powers again in the chow hall. It didn't take long for Robinson to reveal that he had indeed gone across the border into Mexico and had scored some marijuana. I remember feeling my anticipation rise as Robinson laid out a plan for the coming weekend's liberty. We wanted to go as first class as we could afford and get as far away from Camp Pendleton as long as time would allow.

We rented a room in an old hotel in Long Beach, California. During the First World War, this hotel was a first-class place. Now the once expensive carpet was threadbare in places and many of the guests were senior citizens who were permanent residents. Once we unpacked, Powers and I sat around the little table in our room. Robinson produced a 35mm film canister and a very small pipe from his backpack. He took the top off the can and passed it over to Powers and me so we could check out this mysterious green vegetation. To me, it smelled kind of like a hay barn and looked like parsley.

I was eager to find out if what Robinson had said about it was true. Powers, on the other hand, decided at the last minute that this wasn't for him. He was going to stick with his Scotch. He said he came from a long line of drunks and drinking was in his blood, so he was going to stay with his Scotch. Robinson packed the little pipe with this green vegetable matter and showed me how to take a puff and hold it as long as I could. I smoked mentholated cigarettes at the time, but this was different and had a rather pleasant, earthy taste.

Robinson and I smoked a bowlful while Powers sipped his scotch and scrutinized us very closely. Shortly, Robinson plopped on the nearest bed and said in a croaky voice, "Man, this is really good shit," and in return I said something like, "You've got to be kidding me. I don't feel one damn thing." I was waiting for something spectacular, something profound, and I felt nothing. I might as well have smoked some lawn clippings. I know I was feeling a little deflated when Robinson said, "Sometimes this happens on the first time. You're expecting too much, so you don't feel anything." He packed his pipe again and told me to smoke as much as I wanted, until I felt something. I smoked all of it. I held my breath "for as long as I could on every puff" until the bowl was empty. I knocked the ashes out of the pipe and handed it back to Robbie. I still didn't feel any different than when I walked into the room half an hour before. I remember sitting there looking at Powers and his Scotch bottle, thinking that maybe I should have a couple of snorts before we go out on the town.

I walked over to get an empty glass off the counter when I looked out our fifth-floor window. I remember thinking that I hadn't noticed how colorful the neon sign on the hotel across the street looked. I started to feel like I had been in this little room way too long and had a real desire to check out more cool neon signs. I asked Powers what time it was and learned it had been less than forty-five minutes since we walked through the door. I couldn't believe it. It seemed like we had been in the room at least a couple of hours.

Now I was beginning to feel a little suspicious; something was a little different. A very subtle feeling came over me, something totally unexpected—like gentle waves of well-being. The wallpaper was not melting, my head was not spinning, and I was not stumbling around. Throughout this time, Powers was working over his Scotch bottle, and, doing an amazingly accurate W. C. Fields imitation, he complained loudly about how much he hated the Marine Corps issue boxer shorts. He explained in his W. C. Fields voice that real men—where he was from—wear "ball-hugger Jockeys," especially if they were "packing real manly equipment," and that he had brought back "five or six pairs" from boot leave.

As soon as Powers finished his monologue, I said, "Well, let's get the hell out of here." Powers drained his glass and said, "Hell, yeah," and got up off his chair to put on his cool new bell-bottom Levis. When he bent over, I saw that there was a hole the size of a half-dollar in his ball-hugger Jockey shorts, directly over his bung hole. At the moment, I thought it was just about the funniest thing I had ever seen. I couldn't remember ever laughing harder. So, this was it. This was what they were talking about. This was so different from alcohol. I wanted my whole life to feel like this.

My sides still had an unfamiliar ache from laughing so hard as we entered the hotel's old elevator at the end of the hall and headed off on a night of adventure. For a small-town kid who had hardly seen any bright lights, this was a wondrous night of many firsts. We headed down to the Pike, which was one long boardwalk along the beach. The Pike was in its prime operation during the '40s, around World War II, and even into the '50s. But now in 1966, time and weather had given the whole operation an air of being a little crusty around the edges. Rising up from the Pike's carnival atmosphere of tattoo artists, carny games, rides, and amusements was what was once billed as "the world's largest wooden roller coaster."

Two events that evening still stand out in my memory. It was easy to see, even in my altered state, the roller coaster at the Pike was something exceptional, almost otherworldly. I watched in fascination. The old roller coaster had a voice of its own. Thousands of wood beams strained under the pressure of heavy, jerking cars hurtling down the narrow tracks, filled with screaming Saturday night thrill seekers.

Robinson insisted that since this was a night of firsts for me, he and I just had to ride in the front seat. In hindsight, one of the most memorable parts of my first roller coaster ride was the slow trip up the first incline. My eyes strained to take it all in. The lights, the people, the ocean—it was like I was seeing it all for the first time. The rest of the ride was pretty much a blur, except I remember thinking several times that Powers, now a real marine, who was sitting in the seat behind us, made squealing sounds like somebody's little sister.

A little later when our stomachs had settled, we were on a mission to find something good to eat. We rounded a corner and came upon a brightly lit and wildly painted miniature gypsy wagon. The sign next to the wagon said SEE THE CHICKEN PLAY THE PIANO, TEN CENTS. One whole side of the wagon was a window that revealed what was inside: a miniature grand piano on one end and a rather large chicken and a light bulb on the other end. When a rube* deposited a dime in the slot, the light bulb lit up. The chicken then instantly ran across the cage and rapidly pecked on the keys of the piano until the light went off. He then ran back across the cage to an opening that would drop a pellet of chicken feed onto his plate. The three of us probably pumped in five dollars worth of dimes. We ran the chicken absolutely ragged. By the time we had run out of dimes, a large group of laughing people had gathered round us. It was one of those special, unexpected moments in time when a random group of strangers, for whatever reason, briefly let their guard down and laughed and joked together like friends.

Steven James Powers was killed by small arms fire on 2 July 1967 in Quang Tri Provence, Vietnam.

---

* Guys like us

6

During the last week of staging, my battalion participated in a large-scale war games operation. Everyone was being tested to see if they were battle ready. It was hot; it had been all summer. The vegetation in the hills of Camp Pendleton had been baking for months in the California sunshine, and this was an "unusually warm Indian Summer." Before the war games could start everyone had to be in position. Being a 0351 man, I was positioned in a foxhole high up the side of a steep hill. Down in the valley directly across from us was our battalion headquarters encampment. The area was a crossroads, in a convergence of rolling hills. From our foxhole, we had a commanding, almost 180 degree view up both roads, to "protect our command post."

I had gone through boot camp with the guy in the foxhole with me, a marine named Skinner. Before I really got to know Skinner in boot camp I thought if there was a contest between Skinner and our old drill instructor Sergeant Garcia to decide which one was the homeliest, it would be a tough call. Skinner had a visor-like brow, high pronounced cheekbones, a huge chin, and the biggest lips I had ever seen on any human being. Skinner was my first black friend, although he wasn't really black. Skinner told me they called his skin color "mulatto." Skinner came from the ghetto in Chicago and hated rats. The reputed "cat-sized" rats in Vietnam had him worried. He was proud to be a marine. Once I asked Skinner what he did when he went home on boot leave. He told me that he got up every morning, put on his Marine Corps sweatshirt, laced up his boots, bloused his trousers, and ran through the park chanting, "one, two, three, four, I love the Marine Corps."

Skinner had a smile that took up most of his face; it drew you in. You didn't notice the old acne scars or the odd angles of his face. He radiated a gentleness many people don't seem have. Skinner kept his huge smile as he commented on how lucky we were to be in this great foxhole and not humping the scorched hills with the rest of the grunts.

I lit a cigarette and looked over the sandbags. Down in the valley a marine came out of the headquarters tent and popped a red smoke grenade to signal the start of the war games. Almost immediately, smoke and flames burst up in the dry grass around the grenade. At first, watching from our foxhole the entire headquarters company trying to put out the fire with field jackets and E-tools looked like a humorous, almost Keystone cops-style scene.

In an incredibly short period of time, the wind moved the flames across the dry grass and into the dry grease wood and underbrush up the hillside. Before anyone even had a bit of a chance to get control over the fire, it roared up the hill and over the ridge. Later on in the afternoon Skinner and I moved down to the headquarters tent and were told that six marines participating in the war games had been trapped in the fire. Just as we were moving out to join up with our outfit, some desk jockey sergeant came out of the headquarters tent and "volunteered" Skinner to go help pick up the dead marines.

Later that night in a shaky voice, Skinner told me in detail of what bad shape the marines were in. He'd never seen a dead person before. It was one of those life-and-death reality checks. For those of us in Staging Battalion, the sobering reality after the fire was how very quickly the jaws of death can become your reality.

Philip Craig Skinner was killed by machine gun fire near Khe Sanh, 3 May 1967.

In the remaining week of staging, the weather turned cold, and it rained almost nonstop. We pulled a couple more overnight exercises: hiking long distances and eating cold C rations, while being soaked to the bone for most of the time. The general opinion in the ranks—especially among the young unmarried, marines—was that we were totally sick of marching, petty inspections, daily training exercises, and stomping around the hills in Camp Pendleton. Whatever lay ahead, let's just get it over with.

7

O nce I received my Westpac orders, I had to smile. We were all anxious
to get going, and it seemed our government was more than willing
to oblige.

Instead of being packed into the bowels of some navy transport ship
for a month, we were flying on a Continental Airlines jet to Okinawa. I
secretly felt like I had won some kind of personal "lottery ticket." I was
going to fly halfway around the world. Could it get any better than this?
Our final destination didn't even enter my mind.

When we refueled in Hawaii, I traded two packs of Kool cigarettes for
a window seat. For the next nine or ten hours, as my eyes scanned distant
carpets of tinted clouds, I let my mind focus on what my eyes were taking
in, and I consciously tried not to think of anything else.

I think this was the first time I entered into a state of meditation, although
I didn't know it at the time. I do remember feeling exceptionally peaceful.

The jet emerged from the clouds, and the tropical island of Okinawa
appeared as some organic, multishaded green emerald, floating on crystal-
line blue waters. This image viewed through my window was, without a
doubt, the most beautiful and exotic place I had ever seen.

Okinawa was the dispersal hub for marines with Westpac
(Western Pacific) orders. Delay here was usually three to five days while we
received the last of our shots, attended classes on Vietnam, and waited for
orders to our individual units.

At the end of one of our Vietnam indoctrination classes, our old-salt
sergeant instructor—who'd done two tours as a grunt in Vietnam—said in
his most sincere bullfrog voice, "I've got a little word of advice for all you
swinging dicks, especially if you're a grunt. Get drunk, get laid, but before
you do all that, get a steam bath and massage."

I never had a steam bath or a massage before, and neither had the guy who was in the rack above me; I only remember that his nickname was Preacher. Both his parents were evangelical ministers that went from church to church throughout the Southern states. Every member in his quite large family sang and played music.

He hated it.

When he turned eighteen he ran away and joined the Marine Corps. We hit it off right away—probably because of our strong common thread. My grandfather, Leonard Lock, was an Assembly of God minister. While visiting my grandparents over the years, I had met several traveling Evangelical families and made friends with the kids my age.

On our first liberty in Okinawa together, Preacher and I caught a bus into the town of Naha to find, according to our Sergeant instructor, "the best fucking steam bath and massage in town."

We purchased our tickets for $1.75* from a stooped old woman whose skin was the color and texture of a light brown raisin. She was sitting in a brightly lit, elevated glass booth in front of the steam bath. Preacher and I envisioned a large steamy room with a bunch of marines wrapped in white towels, like we had seen in the movies. What we found, however, behind two large, carved wooden doors, was a long corridor with eight or ten doors on the right side. The animated raisin-lady instructed us, with fluttering waves of both hands, that we were to go to the door that had the same number as the number printed on our ticket.

Preacher's room was next to mine, just down the hall. We both hesitated at our doors before entering. I looked over at Preacher as he looked at me. He had this goofy, somewhat fearful grin on his face. I shrugged and said, "What the hell? We already paid for it," and opened the door in front of me.

A rather plain-looking Asian woman, perhaps in her early thirties, motioned to me to strip down and put my clothes on the hooks along the wall. I looked at her and took a back step out into the hall and looked at

---

* Thirty years later I found this ticket at the bottom of my sea bag

Preacher. He had also just taken a back step and was looking at me thinking like, "Oh shit."

The lady in the room then gave an amused laugh and said, "Oh, you cherry boy. Cherry boy you putt close on hook, get an box," pointing to a wooden box just large enough to fit in while seated. Boards that slid to cover the top had a head-hole cut. She was still smiling as she folded her arms and turned away to face the wall. Once I settled my naked self on a small wooden stool in the steam cabinet, so that just my head was sticking out, she wrapped a towel around my neck sealing the gap.

Then "cherry boy" was steamed until cherry red. I felt like I was being scalded like a hog when finally the masseuse opened the steam box for me to climb out. By this time it was modesty be damned, as she guided my wobbly body over to squat on the same very short three-legged milk stool from the steam box now set in the middle of the tile floor. She lathered and scrubbed me from stem to stern with soap and washcloth—nearly. When she finished she extended the soapy washrag, directing it toward my crotch and said, "*doozo*."* With relief from this embarrassment, I washed my own. This soaping was followed with a scrub down all over my body with a bristle brush. She finished the washing part by pouring buckets of water over my entire body rinsing all suds off. She refilled the bucket with hot water dipped from the tub in the floor.

She now guided me to me sit my now very red and naked body in that pool of hot water sunk into the tile floor. I guess you get clean before getting into the bathtub here. I thought I might pass out before she finally pulled me out of this cauldron from hell.

Still dripping wet from the tub, I was directed to climb up on an elevated padded board—a massage table—covered with a clean white sheet. Two large fans, set to blow air across my body, cooled me down fairly quickly.

Following a few minutes of cool-down time, her unbelievably strong hands commenced digging into every muscle in my body including popping finger and toe tips. Finally she climbed up and standing astride

---

* Please, as I understood it, you wash this yourself

me as I was face down on the table reached above her head and grabbed a set of parallel bars. Holding onto them, she increased or decreased her weight while walking up and down my back and legs. Her toes had the power of her fingers.

To this day, I have never had a massage that felt as good as my first one. I know I thought about it at least once a day in the year that followed.

Preacher and I laughed all the way back to base, sharing our mutual experience of being "cherry boys" in an Okinawa steam bath.

Preacher was killed on Hill 881 near Khe Sanh about six months later.

Robinson and I both received orders to go to 2nd Battalion, 3rd Marines, Robbie was going to Golf Company as a grunt, and I was headed to Foxtrot Company's weapons platoon.

The day before we left for Vietnam, everyone with Westpac orders was given early liberty. The enlisted men's bar was opened at 1300 hours. Robinson and I decided to take a hike up into the Okinawa hills. We were going to smoke whatever grass was left in the coveted film canister. We both agreed that mixing pot and combat was probably not a good idea. We had carefully rationed it out over the last weekend liberties, trying to make each time a special experience.

In hindsight, by far the most memorable experiences to come out of Robbie's film canister were the first and the last. Robinson and I rendez-voused at the main gate soon after liberty was called. It didn't take us long to find a trail disappearing into the jungle heading up toward some hills. We hiked a long way, up to a ridge where we found an old concrete Japanese pillbox overlooking the hillside we had just hiked up. Once inside, Robinson and I made ourselves comfortable and ceremoniously smoked up the remainder of the reefer.

In that very quiet moment, although I didn't have a term for it, I felt what the word "vibe" meant. Whatever it was, we both felt it. This was no ordinary place; this place had a feeling to it. We both recalled seeing old newsreels of what happened on Okinawa during World War II. Very few Japanese soldiers survived the battle for Okinawa. Most fought to the death or committed suicide in the final days of the battle. Scores of terrified

Okinawan civilians committed suicide by jumping from the nearby cliffs, in fear of the atrocities the Japanese said the Americans would commit. Here Robinson and I were in this silent Japanese pillbox, in an area where so many died, and tomorrow we were heading into battle. It was like an unsettling religious experience or an overdose of unadulterated reality. We were working our way back down the trail before our communal pipe cooled down.

By the time we made it to the enlisted men's club, it was packed with loud marines slamming down enough twenty-five-cent mixed drinks to last them for least six months. I nursed my twenty-five-cent whiskey sour and looked at the blur of sweaty jarheads.

For the first time, I felt a knot of fear tighten in my stomach. How many of these guys would be going home in a box? Nobody thought it was going to be them. What were the odds of coming home? This was the way it was. This was real. Tomorrow the bullshit was over. Hanging right next to me in the corner of this jam-packed enlisted men's club was a black-metal hanging lamp that had a silhouette of a deer, a tree, and a mountain, with a lit-up, red interior background. The noise in the enlisted men's club seemed to fade the longer I looked at the lamp, and I remember feeling very homesick as it reminded me of the time I lived in McCall, Idaho.

Twelve years later I walked into a bar with no patrons in Mazatlan, Mexico, and saw the same lamp. Even more unsettling was this Mexican bar was laid out similar to the enlisted men's club in Okinawa. I felt like I had stepped into an episode of *The Twilight Zone,* with just me in an empty bar with a very obese Mexican bartender, the lamp, and a flood of young faces from my past washing over me. For years afterward I felt a cold pain in my chest if I let myself remember for too long.

8

Monday, November 28, 1966

My dearest parents,

The day I wrote my last letter, we moved about 10 miles north of Dong Ha. Here we are dug in on a hillside. At night, we can see distant flashes from artillery and the illumination flares. You wouldn't believe the rain. Last night I woke up and I was sleeping in a big puddle. I tried to write before this, but the paper was soggy and tore when I attempted to write on it. The rain has quit for a few hours or so and I have a chance to get a letter out. This is really primitive country. It is not like the jungle you see in Tarzan movies, but very dense shrubs and vines. It takes a little getting used to. I haven't been dry since I got off the plane in Danang.

They have a little village about a mile from our hill. I like to haggle with the shopkeepers. Man talk about salesmanship, I think Dale Carnegie took a course from these people. If you act like you are going to leave, they will jump up and pull you back into their shop, set you back down and lower their price. I bought two bunches of bananas, four bags of peanuts and a pack of Vietnamese cigarettes for a dollar. Not bad for an hour's worth of haggling. If you plan on sending me something for Christmas, send cans of fish or something along that line. Maybe a bag of hard candy. Don't send any pictures until the monsoon season is over. The moisture will just ruin them. Oh yeah, Vikki, you can get busy and send me a box of brownies and my squad leader a box. We share the same tent. We'll both eat them anyway. Corporal David F. Fraley, 21 07728, the rest of the addresses the same as mine. He has been over here for a while and is teaching me things to look out for on patrols. Little hints to keep my butt alive. Vikki, you said you wanted someone to write to, so there it is. Now we are even. How was your Thanksgiving? I sat in a wet bunker eating a can of cold Turkey loaf. Ha. I got turkey too, yeah right.

Love,
John

Corporal Fraley was killed on Hill 881 near Khe Sanh.

From the time I joined F Company, 2nd Battalion, 3rd Marines, we were constantly on the move, running day and night patrols, listening posts, and ambushes. These activities involved different kinds of field operations until we moved up to Camp Carroll. Camp Carroll was a bulldozed plateau that the monsoon rains had turned into an immense red mud pit.

December 6, 1966.

Dear family,

Now I know how old Abe Lincoln felt. Writing by candlelight is for the birds. I'll recap this last week and a half. Our company has really been on the move. Our nickname is "the widow makers." Last Monday, we were heli-lifted into Con Thien, which is 2000 m[eters] from the DMZ. Then we made a sweep back to Cam Lo, which took about eight hours. A sweep is just like an animal hunt. One platoon fans out through an area of jungle flushing out the gooks, meanwhile the other platoons are hidden a couple of miles away. When the aggressor has pushed them through, we pick them off as they run into a clearing. We captured 30 gooks in one sweep. Boy that night I liked to froze to death. In Vietnam, no less, it has been pouring rain for weeks now. Anyway the wind was blowing, and I was soaked and to make things worse when I woke up I was sleeping in a big puddle. All I had to cover up with was a poncho. On the way back we were crunching through the jungle when all of a sudden we came through a clearing and there was a partially destroyed Catholic church with a huge statue of Christ in front. It was covered with moss and the jungle had grown all around it. The chaplain said it probably had been abandoned for 10 years. The French built it when they occupied Indochina. It made me feel sort of small to come on that. It was real beautiful. We got that area secured, and we were going to have it easy for a while. But you know the Marine Corps, dad, we got word that we were moving out at 4:30 a.m . . . You should see this place. It is ankle deep in mud. This is Camp Carroll. I didn't know where the hell I was at first. Trucks stuck, people slipping and falling and busting their butts. We have to clear a couple of areas, which they tell us will take about two months, and then we might go to Okinawa for a rest, and regrouping. God knows this company needs it. I hope everybody is all right. As for me, I am healthy, except that I haven't taken a bath or shower in three weeks, or changed my clothes. I've got blisters, the shits and who knows what else. Oh yes, a runny nose and a sore throat and cough. But so does the whole company. That's what you get for sleeping on the ground for three weeks and eating C rations.

Before we left, I went down to the village and got a haircut. Boy, talk about primitive. They used hand clippers, and an ancient straight razor. For thirty cents, they didn't do too bad a job. They have beautiful little kids around here. There are a million of them. One little boy who couldn't have been over three years old came up to me and said, "Hey Joe, you give me cigarette?" I gave him one, because I thought it was for his old man, or someone like that. He squatted down and lit it up, and started puffing away, inhaling and all. No wonder they are so puny. I am sure homesick, but I guess I'll get over it. Write and tell me about the family. Vikki, remember the brownies? I could use one right now. Well, my candle is about gone and not much space is left, so I'll close for now.

Love,

John

Sometime during December 1966, F Company moved to a position guarding a bridge crossing the Khe Gio River, just Northeast of Camp Carroll on Highway 9. I felt like this was some kind of tropical paradise. We were able to stop for a few days, dig some foxholes, actually have some hot chow, and wash ourselves and our clothes in the river.

December 1966

. . . I was on my 17th Day without a bath or a shave before we came here. I smell like an old wino's socks. I guess I can tell you now that we went on an operation last week. We were going to sweep a village where a suspected company of North Vietnamese Army was in. We moved all night and by daybreak we moved in, but they had detected us, and not a soul was there. Boy, were we mad. That meant we had to carry all those rounds back that night. Twelve of us stayed behind to set up an ambush. We were set in at a crossroads. I had first watch for my position. All of a sudden several dozen shots were fired. Man, it scared the hell out of me. It was just a water buffalo that charged the position just down from me. Those things weigh two tons and are meaner than hell. The sun broke through yesterday and I got sunburned. It's cloudy again today. Last night was pretty hairy. My foxhole is on top of a steep, steep mountain. About three in the morning, some of those army assholes started firing a quad 40 mm cannon at us. They got their wires crossed and started blowing the hell out of our hill. It was pretty hairy all right. A lieutenant in one of the rifle platoons was hit pretty bad, and had to be medevaced out that night. The Medevac pilot exhibited amazing skills. The grunts were only able to hack out a small clearing in the bush, about 20 yards from where we were dug in, so I had an incredible ringside seat. In the middle of the night, on the side of a steep jungle covered mountain, in the pouring rain, he was able to rescue that wounded Marine. In the morning we did a little recon into the jungle to see where they had hit, and guess what we found? A helicopter that had been shot down probably over a year ago. Now there is a whole bunch of brass inspecting the wreckage. They haven't found any bodies as of yet. Say Sis how about a sack of hard candy or something. Oh yeah, tell dad to buy a Playboy each month, read it and send it to me. I really dig the articles in that magazine. Well, I've got to take a bath in the river, so I must close. I wish you all a Merry Christmas and I hope we can spend next Christmas together.

Love,
John

9

We had about ten days on the river where we had set up our perimeter around the bridge. We did run a few patrols and listening posts, but for the most part we had some much-appreciated downtime. We could get our gear squared away, write letters home, and let our jungle rot and blisters heal. Around that time I was no longer the company's FNG, so I became acquainted with some of the marines outside my squad.

One particular marine who I liked immediately and whose company I enjoyed any time I could get around him was a rifleman named Lance Corporal Arthur Vigil. Art Vigil's life and mine intertwined many times in the coming months. This is some of his background as I remember: Vigil was an old salt of three months or so when I met him. He had seen a little combat in operation "Hastings," I believe. He was dark-haired, about 5'10", had broad shoulders, and was well-built. He had been a professional soccer player who was a member of a prestigious Danish soccer team and was playing in Denmark when he was drafted.

When Art got his draft notice, he brought his girlfriend—also the soccer team's English interpreter, named Judy Poli—to the United States to live with his family while Art went into the Marines. Art would amaze me with his soccer skills. I had never played a soccer game in my life. Many times he would break the tension or entertain a throng of Vietnamese kids by bouncing his soccer ball off his knees, to his head, to his elbows, off his hip, to the side of his foot, and back to his head.

Over the years, I have come to think of Art as a toned-down version of Robin Williams. He always had this upbeat way about him. Art had an uncanny ability to sense where people were "coming from." If they were down or depressed, within five minutes he could have that person falling on the floor with laughter. It didn't matter if the story was all that funny—he was a master at delivery.

As an example, one long and rather miserable night on a listening post, Art told me a story with plenty of detail about his hometown best friend Axel, whose pride and joy was a 1960 Cadillac. The nutshell version is that he and Axel went to the store in Axel's Caddy. As they were leaving the parking lot, Axel backed up over an old lady and broke her leg. There is nothing funny about any part of the story, but the way Art told it, I thought it was just hysterical. It was all I could do to hold back the laughter that would have given away our position.

The Khe Gio River was a tropical paradise. We could wash our clothes and swim when we weren't on patrol or on some work detail. Peaceful, almost normal, swimming in the river, laughing, but not quite. The war was still hiding in the trees at the water's edge. I was ever vigilant, my eyes always scanning the jungle. Every once in a while when none of the brass were around, someone would throw a grenade into the river to help some of the local kids downstream. They weren't allowed to come close to us, but occasionally a group would gather downstream on the other side of the river and call out "Marines number 1, VC number 10."* The grenade-aided dead fish would float downstream, and there would be a scramble of kids swimming out to retrieve them.

Camp Carroll was a pretty rough place in mid-December 1966, when we moved up from the river. F company was in charge of occupying a line of bunkers and guarding the southwest perimeter of Camp Carroll. To our northeast, the army had an artillery emplacement, with 105 mm, 155 mm, and 175 mm guns. The 175 mm has a range of over twenty miles and shoots a projectile about as long as my leg. If the army had a night-firing mission, the concussion was so tremendous that it blew out the candles in our tents and bunkers. Camp Carroll was a raw wound gouged out on the top of a jungle plateau.

As primitive as Camp Carroll was, it felt almost civilized to me; we had been out in the bush for nearly a month. Camp Carroll had hot chow, real shitters with doors on them, and something totally new for

---

* Number 1, very good, VC (Viet Cong) number 10, very bad.

me called a piss tube. A piss tube was an artillery canister that was sunk into the ground at an angle where you could just step up and take a leak. I had been carrying a "piss tube" around for a month and hadn't made the connection.

Camp Carroll was named after a young captain, J. J. Carroll, who was killed taking the ground that bears his name. In the year that I was based there, I often wondered who J. J. Carroll was. Many years later, in the mid-'90s, I met a retired marine officer who had gone through officer candidate school with J. J. Carroll and had been a close friend. He told me Carroll was a marine's marine. He could howl at the moon all night, drink everyone under the table, and still be the most outstanding marine in the morning inspection.

They pulled us from the field and back up to Camp Carroll on the afternoon of Christmas Eve. It hadn't stopped raining in the five days we had been out. My feet were a mess; they looked like some kind of white cheese. I had run out of dry socks about midway through the patrol. It felt like my feet were on fire during the long slog up the back side of the plateau to Camp Carroll. The thing that sticks in my mind, besides my feet, was that when we reached the top of the plateau in the back of a 4x4 there was a black, almost purple, Santa Claus, with the red hat and coat and white beard, handing out Red Cross packages. I had never even thought about an African American Santa Claus. I remember thinking, *how odd, a black Santa Claus*. Well, like the old salt said, "only in Vietnam." Everyone made good use of the day and a half that we had back at Camp Carroll. Mostly we ate and slept, tended our feet, and wrote letters.

Mid-December,

Camp Carroll

Pardon the smudges, but it can't be helped. The mud is calf high and that is on the road. Yesterday I came back from another patrol; that's when I picked up the propaganda sheets. They drop them along the trails from the air. The colored one is an open arms pass to any North Vietnamese who wants to defect to our side. The others are self-explanatory. Now this I know you won't believe. There is a large trench that is used to prevent flooding around our tents. You can imagine what color the water is. We washed our clothes in the trenches and got most of the chunks of the mud off of them. That day they were burning out the shitters to prevent the maggots from multiplying. The shitters are 30 gallon drums cut in half and then filled with six or 8 inches of diesel oil. They are regular looking out houses made of plywood, most with two seats. In the back of the outhouse there is a door where you can slide the drums in under the seat. Every couple of days, some lucky individuals are selected to join the "burn the shitters work party," which includes pulling the drums out, burning all of fecal material until it is ash, cleaning them out, refilling them with diesel, and then putting them back. The reason for all this detail is this: Once we had washed our utilities* in the trench, if one stood up wind of a burning shitter, one could dry out his jungle utilities in a matter of minutes. Even upwind, the smell could get pretty intense. They came out bone dry and as stiff as a board, as if they had been starched. If you look on a map you can see where I am. We are about 20 miles north of Dong Ha. Yep, we are almost on that line. Yesterday the company next to us killed four VC right in camp. They were stealing weapons and food, they are sneaky little turds. The country is very mountainous around here, and the jungle, man, when I am on patrol it looks like a Tarzan flick; vines, plants, bamboo, strange jungle noises. PAUL, THE CORPS SUCKS! STAY OUT! I am sorry that I can't send any Christmas presents, but we can't even go down into the village anymore or buy things from the gooks, they are a little nasty. They can booby-trap anything. Sometimes I have a feeling they don't like me very well. When I get some letters, I'll have to burn them. If the enemy finds old letters, they have been known to write nasty letters home . . .

Love

John

The company moved back out into the bush the day after Christmas. It was good to get out of the field even if it was just for that short while. All of us had a hot meal on Christmas Eve, and it was a good opportunity to dry out our feet and our socks. The rain had been relentless for days on end. We moved north, on the northwest side of Camp Carroll, and down into a valley with several small villages, a few rice paddies and lots of bush. We moved until almost nightfall and then made a perimeter; everyone dug in.

---

*   Clothing

Almost immediately our foxholes started filling up with water. We had to keep scooping the water out of our hole with our helmets. Just sitting there in the pouring rain, looking out at the pitch black, feeling chilled to the bone, and the relentless rain beating incessantly on my helmet made me feel even more miserable. Sometime in the middle of the night, as I stared out into the black trying to keep from shivering, I saw movement coming my way in the darkness, and I called out a challenge. It turned out to be a squad leader from one of the rifle companies, checking the lines. He was Corporal James Moses. I had seen him around and had talked to him a couple of times. He stayed and talked to us for a few minutes. Some of what he said was about missing his wife and kids around Christmas. Corporal Moses didn't smoke, but before he left to check the rest of the line, he gave us a dry, four-pack of C ration Pall Malls that he retrieved from inside his helmet. What a treat.

As Blevins stood watch, I made a tent out of my poncho by pulling my head through the hole, squatted down deep into the foxhole, and fired up a dry cigarette. Of all the cigarettes I smoked in my life none are more memorable than the dry Pall Malls I smoked that night in a foxhole. Thank you, Corporal Moses. Here was a man with a good heart, who had picked up our spirits. His little gesture did a lot for our morale. All Blevins and I needed at the time was a good word and a dry smoke.

On the morning of December 27, we broke camp early and moved through the valley over old rice paddies and through areas of low jungle, trying to flush out the enemy. As it turned out, they were just ahead of us and moving fast. In the early afternoon our company pulled off to the side of the trail for a break. Word came down that they wanted a couple of fire teams to recon the area up ahead. Naturally every FNG in the company got picked. As we moved out, we got a little static from some of the "old salts" like, "I'll smoke another cigarette for ya," or "Go get 'em tiger, I'm going to take a little nap." That kind of thing.

Our little scouting mission moved along a tree-lined trail, then out along a series of old rice paddies with fairly high banks. Ahead, next to the rice paddies, was the steep jungle-covered northwest wall of the valley. Just as we were getting ready to turn around and head back toward the company, several automatic weapons opened up on us from somewhere up on the side of the mountain. We immediately dove for cover behind one of the rice paddy walls. I remember thinking, *Shit, these are real bullets flying over my head. Oh man, someone is shooting directly at me.* We returned fire. I emptied several magazines of ammunition from my M-14 to where I thought the fire was coming from. *I'm shooting at another human being!* No hesitation, no problem, we all opened up. Most all of us on that patrol were the newer guys in the company—this was our first firefight.

Fire suppression was yet to be in our vocabulary, and we lay down an impressive field of fire. We radioed the company that we had made contact, not that they couldn't hear our call. It was actually quite enjoyable to watch all those guys, who were napping or having that second cigarette just for me fifteen minutes ago, double-timing to our position.

> From my notebook:
> The NVA are pretty smart, more than pretty smart sometimes. If you trap them, or get them blocked into a Valley, and you have the Old Green Machine fumble fucking around with each other . . . trying to coordinate several grunt companies, the NVA will usually decide that it's not advisable to a engage us, and disappear over the ridge line.

After a few moments to catch their breath, fire a few rounds, and formulate a game plan, the 1st Squad, led by Corporal Moses, moved out of the rice paddy, and disappeared into the thick undergrowth and up the side of the steep mountain. Ten minutes later, the NVA opened up on them—even before the last man in the company had moved out of the rice paddy. About a hundred yards from the rice paddy the terrain became so severe, and the jungle was so thick, the only way to move forward was to work our way up a sheer, rocky creek bed. When the firing started everyone took cover behind whatever rock was in front of them. It only lasted twenty seconds or so, and then it was all quiet. A few minutes later the word was getting passed down the line, "They're moving a body down the creek."

The marines further up the creek from me started sliding Corporal Moses' body back down the creek bed. Up ahead I heard someone say,

"He's going to be all right." As I helped slide him on down past me, I saw a hole in his temple, no bigger than the diameter of a pencil, with a little bit of fat hanging out of it, and I knew he wasn't going to be all right. *He's dead.* I remember thinking *How can this be? He has a wife and kids. This guy can't be dead. He was a nice guy, he didn't deserve this.* A couple of days later they pulled us back to the rear at Camp Carroll. We had been on the move for five hard days, in heavy rain. We were exhausted and most of the company had some degree of trench foot—large chunks of dead white skin, on the bottom of the feet, peeling off in layers.

10

January 11, 1967

My Loved Ones,

This place can get very dull, so I'll recap the past week's events. Today the corpsman took the core out of my boil without any painkiller. As he started, I saw the lieutenant cringe, and I knew I wasn't going to be crying. He drained about a pint (I'm exaggerating) of pus out of my heel from an infected blister, so I'm on light duty for a week. This country is full of diseases. Small cuts can turn into something serious if not taken care of. Today when I was guarding the rear gate, a small band of villagers approached the checkpoint, men women and children. As I inspected them, I couldn't help but think maybe some of them are Vietcong, but they could also be innocent farmers. This is what makes this conflict so difficult. You don't actually know who your enemy is until he fires at you. In the meantime, many harmless farmers are killed. Their farms and animals are destroyed by both sides. It is no wonder that many of them resent us being here. I probably could get court-martialed for saying this, but I too am against this war. Simply because it isn't a war; it is a political fiasco, put on by high officials for their personal gain and benefit. We can have this thing over in six months if they would let us. Instead we are always on the defensive instead of the aggressive. We could wipe them all out if we were able to use the equipment that is supposed to be backing us. But no, we are running trivial patrols and getting little results. Only when the NVA or local VC hit us, do we make some effort to do some fighting. It is not the men here, but rather the men and people in the United States, keeping the war going. The stock market is booming once again. Politically speaking, jobs are more secure than ever, and all important, the majority of the people in the United States, unless they are personally connected with someone over here, could care less what happens. In short, we have no backing. And the individuals directly related with the war will profit more the longer it lasts. We came over here with good intentions and started off well, but now we are making a mockery of the American government, the American people, and the American Constitution. No wonder we are hated by other countries that we've occupied. We make one blunder after another. The only way to win the war is to win the people. Our people-to-people program here, from what I've

49

seen, has failed, not particularly because it is our fault. Some people just can't be friendly to people they aren't sure of. The same guy you give a cigarette or candy to that day could be waiting in ambush that night. There must be some way to end this war, but as I see it, it will cost lots more lives and sorrow before someone wises up. I didn't mean to get so carried away, but I have a strong love for my country and I hate to see it being degraded this way.

Love,

John

* * * *

In January, our company moved back down to the bridge crossing the Khe Gio River just north of Camp Carroll on Highway 9, and we stayed here all of January, and into the middle of February. We ran many operations and patrols, manned listening posts and set up ambushes. We were making sporadic contact with elements of 324 and 326B of the North Vietnamese regulars. Sometimes we would catch fire while on patrols. Occasionally they would hit us at the bridge. It was nothing you'd call heavy combat, just mostly a lot of humping up and down very steep hills, during hot steamy days and crouching down through long, chilly, wet nights in the jungle, at ambush positions or listening posts.

Some days when there were no operations and nothing going on, we did have a chance to clean our gear, write letters home, make elaborate cups of hot chocolate, and catch up on sleep. We smoked a lot of cigarettes, and listened to music on transistor radios down by a bend in the river where there was a nice place to take a swim. Even though we lived in a hole surrounded by several rows of sandbags, this was a tropical paradise compared with some of the places the company bivouacked.

There are two incidents during this time that that stand out in my memory. The traffic on Highway, 9 whether it was a convoy or a single jeep or tank, always drove faster along this road to keep from being an easy target, except on the bridge. Across the bridge, the road took a sharp left, following the contour of the river along a sheer mountainside.

One afternoon, as I was sitting on the thick sandbag wall in front of my bunker, reading a coveted copy of *Time* magazine, I looked up and watched a tank slowly cross the bridge. The tank then resumed speed as it returned to the dirt road. Just as it approached the sharp left bend, a Jeep with two marines came around the corner in the opposite direction, and in an instant the tank ran over them. After seeing there was no helping the Jeep occupants, the tank crew hooked onto the flattened remains and dragged it to the nearby company headquarters tent with the bodies still inside.

Oh man, I tried not to look in that direction. I went out of my way to stay away from it until a group of officers and a few medical types came from the plateau. And after a long discussion, they finally put the remains in body bags and left. It was late the next day before someone came to pick up what was left of the Jeep. There was going to be some kind of investigation. When I finally had to walk past the crushed Jeep, I could still see chunks of flesh ground into the metal. It was truly gruesome and sobering. Later, as I had to walk past that mangled mess again, the old-salt corporal walking next to me said, "Well, you know, fuck 'em—I'm glad it wasn't me."

This was the beginning of an understanding of what I felt was "battlefield gratitude." At first his words shocked me like a bucket of cold water, until I thought about it. He was right . . . I was sorry for the two mangled marines, and I was truly thankful it wasn't me. That kind of thought numbs you to the core. I knew what I saw, but I didn't. I could feel only so much, only allow in so much.

Since the first of the year, the scuttlebutt was that 2nd Battalion, 3rd Marines was going to Okinawa some time in late February or early March. The Marine Corps would rotate one of its battalions after so many months in the field. The battalions that had "hit a lot of shit," would be sent back to Okinawa. Once there the battalion would get resupplied with new guys, new equipment, train a little, and then return to Vietnam.

The time had finally come. The Okinawan dream was becoming a reality for everyone. You could hear it in their voices; long patrols didn't seem so far, and the packs didn't seem so heavy. Combat-wise, during the last week, we didn't do anything major. However, on my last patrol I remember an incident—the second incident that made a lasting impression.

The mountains around the bridge were extremely steep, and we were patrolling an area we had been over many times. Our ten-man patrol started out before light, worked our way up to a ridge line, and by late afternoon we completed a wide circle almost back down to the road where we started. We were all hot and pretty well spent physically. The vision of plunging into the river quickly faded, however, when an NVA soldier opened up on us with his AK-47 from the ridge line, emptying a magazine at us down in the valley below. He missed us. Not a single grunt was hit. But we reported that we were under fire.

Headquarters radioed back that we should go back up on the ridge and check it out. Well, we all knew that the guy was long gone. More than likely we had walked right by him in some practically invisible spider hole just off the trail. This was a particularly steep and rocky area, and climbing back up to that ridge line would have just been terrible.

Leading our patrol was a rather large staff sergeant named Stone. Stone passed down the line that everyone should spread out, get off the trail and out of sight in the elephant grass, and keep the smoking lamp out. For the next two hours, the sergeant radioed in fake radio reports, eventually indicating that we had made no contact with the enemy. Everyone kept their mouths shut when we walked back in.

It was the first time I was ever a part of something not done by the book. I was as happy as the rest of the guys on the patrol that we didn't go back up on the ridge line, but there was an aspect, too, about lying that didn't sit well with me.

February 17, 1967

My Dear Family,

I told you about Delta Five, an ARVN* outpost. Well, we spent just one night there. That night I stood watch wrapped in my poncho with a shivering ARVN beside me. Although about 3 a.m., we got word to move out and we did just that. So six days later I get all my back mail and we have a chance to

---

* The Army of the Republic of Vietnam

write. What a miserable operation . . . I am about to make an important decision. I was asked if I'd like to become a sniper, since I'm an expert shot. I think I'd make a good one, and I would like to get out of rockets. I will make my mind up after we get back from Okinawa. Anyway, that's what I told the company commander; he saw me dinging them in there at target practice. So, time will tell. I am going to church. It's held outside and just a few of us go. I took communion for the first time in almost a year. Last time I took it was when I visited Pop in Elko. It seems like such a long time ago and yet not a year has passed. . . .

Love,
John

On February 26, we were declared an inactive fighting unit, and the battalion started making preparations for our big move. The mood around our company was almost as if everyone was waiting for a special Christmas. No one talked about anything else; hot chow from a real mess hall, clean sheets, steam baths and massages, movies and ice cream, mixed drinks for twenty-five cents in the enlisted men's club, not to mention many colorful discussions about where the best bar girls were in Naha.

Like the line in the old song, "What a difference a day makes."

11

In the early afternoon, a convoy of trucks rolled up alongside the road by the bridge. The company tents were struck, and all of our equipment was loaded into 4x4s. That night there was almost a sense of euphoria on the line; little parties in the sandbag bunkers with shared cigarettes and pictures and gourmet hot chocolate in canteen cups. A marine in the bunker down from us shared a long-hoarded bottle of Suntory Japanese whiskey, stashed away from his last R&R. There were faint notes of the Beatles and *the Little Rascals* from Armed Forces radio drifting down the river and on into the jungle darkness.

It was close to 0400 when I was woken out of a deep sleep. At first I thought I was still dreaming—what I was hearing couldn't be true. "Grab my shit and head for the trucks? We're going into the field?" What? For about five seconds, I thought someone was pulling some bullshit. "No bullshit, marine—real deal!"

It is my understanding of the events unfolding then, from information I have gathered over the years, that our overall situation was this: A company of Ninth Marines on a sweep operation was moving up to replace us at the bridge. Our old nemesis, elements of 324, or 326B of the NVA regulars set the bait in a trap, by surrounding one of the 9th Marines recon units, a couple miles northeast of Cam Lo.

At that time, the NVA could have easily overrun their position, but left enough marines alive to call for help. A reinforced company of 9th Marines, escorted by a tank, went to rescue them. Now they themselves were surrounded and sustaining heavy casualties. The battle was taking place about ten miles south of us, several hundred meters off the road.

The word came down from the colonel that this was going to be our last hurrah before Okinawa. We were going in—rescue those marines— give a little payback to the NVA, and then do a sweep back to the road and the waiting trucks. I believe the colonel thought this was a personal gift from the war gods. "Every swinging dick is going into the field" meant all of the office pogues, cooks, armorers, even the chaplain and his assistant.

The trucks stopped a few miles north of Dong Ha, and we disembarked just as it was getting light. We headed east from the road at a double time. I barely got started when I had what only could be called an extremely memorable sense of reality or awareness.

A couple of weeks before, I had been promoted to gunner. I remember feeling a little puffed up by it. I even wrote home and told my folks that I had been issued a .45 caliber pistol. Only officers, corpsman, and gunners are issued .45s. Now I am double-timing into a real battle, feeling like the obvious bull's-eye in my group. Here I am lugging a rocket launcher, with two white-phosphorous rockets strapped to my backpack, and only a .45 pistol for my personal protection. I had moved only a short distance when the sounds of a large battle began.

I couldn't help thinking of stories about rocket men who were nearly vaporized after the rockets they were carrying took a hit. About this time, Weapons Platoon moved to the side of the trail and let the riflemen from Golf Company move up to the front. Automatic gunfire seemed much closer and more frequent now. I lit a cigarette, and the thoughts of being vaporized vanished when I made eye contact with my good friend Harold Robinson, double-timing to the front. He gave me a big smile and thumbs up, and of course I gave it back like, "Hell yeah." But there was something in his face and probably something behind mine.

At eighteen or nineteen, every boot marine felt nothing bad was going to happen to him. You leave boot camp with a sense of immortality, having no real concept of what a life-and-death situation is. I saw how quickly those marines were burned alive at Camp Pendleton or run over by a tank or shot like Corporal Moses; I realized that this was going to be something like that. People are going to die here—that is the unspoken reality. "Good luck, Robbie," I thought, as he double-timed past me. Maybe being in weapons platoon wasn't so bad after all.

By the time I made it to the battle site, the riflemen had established a perimeter around a long-abandoned rice paddy. The rice paddy was shaped like a very thick C, with dense jungle surrounding the back edge. There was only sporadic small arms fire at that time.

Weapons Platoon was ordered to take up positions on a rocky tongue of land (the inside of the C) and dig in, while they medevaced out the 9th Marines casualties. As I moved into position, the first thing I saw was a blown-out American tank. *Oh shit, this is not good.* There was a dead marine lying in the fork of the trail, facedown. My thought was that he was made out of translucent china, his skin was so white. Then, I started seeing bodies all over, dead and wounded marines, and dead NVA.

Trying to dig in proved to be very difficult and scary. The ground was hard and rocky, and about every 30 seconds, a couple of mortar rounds would explode nearby, causing everyone to dive for cover. We were digging hard and fast, but our hole was less than a foot deep when a very close explosion caused us to hit the deck again. A couple of riflemen about ten yards on down from us spotted a well-camouflaged NVA artillery forward observer hiding in the bush. From his position the NVA soldier was able to see where we were located and call in our position to the NVA mortar emplacement. One rifleman threw a frag* in on him. And one of these riflemen, I don't remember who, called to me, "Hey Nutting, come check this shit out."

They had pulled the NVA soldier out to the trail by the time I made it down to them. He was lying on his back and still breathing; the concussion of the grenade had knocked him out. I stood over him and looked down in his face. I saw that his teenage face had multiple tiny wounds from the fragmentation wire. I had never seen the face of the enemy— not alive and up close. What made this experience so extremely profound for me is that the NVA soldier looked remarkably similar to a Japanese friend I had when I was a kid in Twin Falls, Idaho. He didn't look like the enemy I had pictured in my mind; this guy looked about sixteen, very slight build with thick black hair—and yet there he was, a uniformed NVA soldier.

---

* Hand grenade

While I was standing there looking at him, he appeared to be waking up. At the same time, a lieutenant and two squad leaders came up from behind to see what the hell was going on. I guess I didn't hear the lieutenant the first time, but I sure did the second time when he yelled at me, "I said, shoot that motherfucker, Private!" and he was looking right at me.

Here I am, the guy with the .45 pistol, and I'm standing over a uniformed enemy, who only moments before had been calling in mortar rounds on my fellow marine. I have just been given a direct order by an officer to kill an enemy. I undid my holster and had just pulled out my .45, when one of the squad leaders, Corporal Fyte, stepped in around me and put three rounds from his M-14 into the NVA's head.

I have no doubt that I would have carried out the lieutenant's order. I also have no doubt that had I done so, I would've been haunted by the memory for the rest of my life. I've always thought of Corporal Fyte with a sense of gratitude. I don't know why he did it; maybe he knew I was an FNG, or maybe he saw something in my face.

We didn't receive any more incoming mortar or small arms fire during the time it took to medevac the ninth Marines.

We moved out of the rice paddy and into thick jungle. I understood the plan was to do a wide sweeping maneuver around the rice paddy and maybe catch "a few stragglers," on the way back to the waiting trucks. Being a rocket man, my position was toward the end of a long column that headed down the trail and into double-canopy bush.

The canopy blocked out much of the light and the bush felt way too close. Lugging the 0351, I felt like a big, impotent neon target. About a hundred yards down the trail, off to the left, was an abandoned NVA camp. There was a helmet and backpack, a water jug, and some kind of cookware around a campfire that had died out. It was booby-trapped for sure. It was the first time I had seen something like it. I had moved just past this little camp and into some real thick vegetation when all hell broke loose.

The NVA had set up what amounted to a battalion-sized ambush and we walked into it. In the clearings, they opened up not only with small arms fire but preregistered mortar rounds and rocket-propelled grenades. Along the trail ahead were strategically placed spider traps. The initial fire was so intense they were able to completely cut off some of the front elements almost immediately.

The word came down to pull back and make a perimeter. I moved back to the west end of the rice paddy, close to where the trails intersected, and found a nice deep foxhole to dive into, behind a small rise in the ground. The encompassing sounds of battle were everywhere, explosions, cries, and bullets cracking over my head.

I didn't see another person. I was in a foxhole hole all by myself, with this battle going on all around me, and I didn't see anybody. I'm thinking to myself, only last week I first heard the term "screwed the pooch" when a marine was talking about a particularly bad situation he had been in. I'm thinking I must be "screwing the pooch" here, because I won't be able to hold this position for long with a .45 caliber pistol and a couple of magazines. I stashed the 0351 and the white phosphorous rockets down in the foxhole.

I made sure there was a round chambered in my .45 and looked over the edge. I saw a rifleman running hard toward me, zigzagging like a football player, and then he dove into my foxhole. His name was Walter Smith, "Smitty," and he was a football player. As I found out later, he was a well-known high school football star from Hamilton, Montana.

Smith was all bloody. He had a gunshot wound through his right forearm. He had a large chunk of skin missing from the back of his neck and multiple smaller wounds in his back caused by a mortar round.

By the time I got the bleeding stopped, I had used up both our supplies of bandages. Walt kept protesting about me using my bandages on him. We were told in training, the reason you carry bandages is for yourself, not for the other guy. I told Walt that I had read this section in the Marine Corps handbook about if someone is shooting at you, you're supposed to hit the deck. So, with foxhole humor I said I probably wouldn't need any bandages, but since he was from Montana, we should probably find him a few extras.

From the sounds of things, both Walt and I were convinced that the entire North Vietnamese Army was getting ready to break through the jungle, right in front of our position. Because of the gunshot wound through his forearm, now Smitty was unable to hold his rifle, so we swapped his M-14 rifle for my .45 caliber pistol. I felt a sense of relief at having an M-14 rifle between me and the nearby enemy.

My relief instantly evaporated, however, when a white-haired gunnery sergeant came by our foxhole looking for volunteers. He was looking for any unwounded riflemen to go back down the trail and see if we could help any of the wounded get back to our perimeter. He had this look on his face that caught my attention. I hadn't seen it before.*

The gunny's voice sounded a little airy when he said, "I'm not going to ask you to go back up that trail. This is voluntary." He also said, "You can hear what those fuckers are doing to our guys out there." I didn't really even think about it. I took Walt's rifle and ammunition and went with him. I joined up with two other marines on the trail. One was a stout marine named PFC Bean; the other was my old rocket partner, Blevins.

We had to work our way across a somewhat open area that had a fairly gentle rise in the ground. We were almost where the trail entered the dense jungle when someone called to us. It was our colonel; he was propped up against a tree. He had a large battlefield dressing on his leg and crotch. Lying next to him, wrapped in a poncho, was our severely wounded first sergeant.

We reported to the colonel, and we told him we were going back in for the wounded. He said something about keeping our heads down—move fast—don't stop—good luck. Blevins headed up the trail first, then me, and then Bean.

Blevins was flying up the trail, and I was matching him step for step. As we reached the edge of the jungle, small-arms fire struck around us with increased intensity. With all the rifle fire, there was no way to tell where it was coming from. We were about fifty yards past the abandoned NVA campsite when a mortar round landed just in front of us. I dove for cover

---

* I later learned on the hospital ship the term for that look: "fucking, stone-cold fear, man"

off the side of the trail. It was then that Blevins and I discovered that Bean wasn't behind us. We were turning around to go back and look for him when he caught up with us. He was a little out of breath and said something like he wasn't able to "run as fast as you fucking guys."

This was no place for a discussion. We decided we would go as fast as Bean, so he took point, then Blevins, then me. I had moved about two steps when a mortar round landed behind us, right where we just were. The concussion blew me off my feet, and shrapnel penetrated my right lower leg. Blevins was hit in the shoulder and in the side of the head; shrapnel missed Bean altogether. We had to turn back.

Bean got through this battle unscathed and went back to Okinawa with the battalion. He died on Hill 861, near Khe Sahn, trying to clear a jam in his newly acquired M-16 rifle.

The first thing Walt Smith did when I saw him in the triage area was laugh out loud. "I told ya, I told ya so, and you said there was no way you were going to get hit."

"Fuck you, Smitty, twice," I said.

The word came down that everybody who was wounded was being medevaced out and those who could should move down to the clearing. The battle seemed to be going on all around those of us in the triage area, but the word was the colonel was bleeding to death, and he had to be medevaced ASAP.

I was lying up on the side of mound, several yards away from our first sergeant, when the first medevac helicopter came in. Walt had moved down to the edge of the rice paddy with a group of the more ambulatory wounded. It all happened so fast.

The medevac pilot attempted to land in the rice paddy, and suddenly the air filled with the sounds like ten thousand rifles shooting at once. The pilot tried to abort the mission and gain altitude. He had cleared the rice paddy and was just over the edge of the jungle when the helicopter exploded into a ball of fire. For several seconds the firing ceased, and I heard one of the wounded up the hill say, "Oh fuck. We're not getting out of here."

I know our first sergeant heard it too. He kind of gurgled and moaned and tried to roll on his side, and then he just quit breathing. I can't remember his name. He was a large Mexican. He had a big family and had been in the Marine Corps for over twenty years. He and the colonel had been hit in the initial barrage on Headquarters Company. A mortar or RPG had amputated his legs at the knees, one arm was badly damaged, and his chin was almost gone.

By late afternoon the battalion was in serious trouble. We were running out of ammunition on the line and we had sustained many casualties. The colonel was barely hanging on by a thread. One last attempt was made to rescue him, and whatever wounded they could. A Chinook helicopter came in from the east, fast and low, and was almost able to land within a few meters to the edge of the rice paddy where several corpsmen, Walt, the colonel, and ten or twelve other wounded were.

From my vantage point, back up on the side of the mound where most of the wounded were spread out, the fire that erupted from the bush was almost like a movie. Rounds were striking everywhere, kicking up dirt and debris. An RPG came across the rice paddy, narrowly missing the helicopter. It exploded in the tree line behind the group of wounded. The pilot immediately aborted the mission and began to take off.

A Chinook helicopter has two large rotors, with a huge capacity for troops or supplies. Loading is generally through a ramp in the rear that is lowered. The Chinook has another troop door on the right side of the fuselage, where a door gunner usually mans an M-60 machine gun.

About the time the RPG exploded, Walt took off like somebody had shot a starter's pistol at a track meet. Before the helicopter had lifted off no more than a couple feet, Walt had covered the distance—with bullets flying all around him—and jumped up, grabbing a hold of the edge of the rear ramp of the rising helicopter. I watched in disbelief as the helicopter continued to rise, lifting him higher and higher. Being shot through the forearm, he was not going to be able to hold on very long. As the helicopter banked to the right, I could see Walt being pulled in. Later, Walt said the door gunner told him he "saw his white knuckles and pulled his ass in."

The helicopter was carrying much-needed ammunition for the marines below, so while the door gunner was pushing out several crates of ammo to the grunts in the field, Walt fired the M-60 machine gun into the surrounding NVAs, as the helicopter circled back overhead. He said he could see NVA all over the place. Unfortunately, one of the ammunition crates landed on a marine below and killed him.

As far as I know, Walt was the only maine in our battalion to get out of there that night. Walt said he was treated like royalty once they flew him back to Danang. They had a whole field hospital on standby waiting for all the casualties. Walt said he had majors and colonels working on his wounds, calling him "son" and asking him many questions, hungry for details of the battle. The "cherry on the cake" for Walt that night was a big bowl of ice cream after a hot meal.

For the rest of the battalion, nightfall came, with the sounds of small arms fire escalating and diminishing around us, continuous without letup. During the night we heard the screams of a marine tortured in the darkness.

Puff the Magic Dragon—a converted Air Force C-47—spewed bullets with three 7.62 mm General Electric machine guns. I was told that in less than three seconds this gun, shooting so rapidly, could deliver a single round in three square yards in the area the size of a football field. Every fifth round was a tracer; the view was like seeing a red waterfall just appearing out of the black sky. All night long, parachute flares swung down on our position, giving every object eerie, dancing shadows.

Then, several hours after dark, the NVA made a major push. The only thing that saved us that night was the army artillery from Camp Carroll. For most of the night, the 105 mm and the 155 mm guns shot fire missions around our perimeter with outstanding accuracy.

What a surreal experience—seeing all of the red tracer bullets and the eerie dancing light from the pyrotechnics, hearing the distinctive sounds of automatic rifle fire and incoming artillery rounds. Many times the American army shells exploded close enough to blow fist-sized chunks of sod on me.

Sometime in the middle of the night, a corpsman came and checked on me. I recognized him—he was a skinny Mexican corpsman with a big smile. I'm fairly certain he was from Golf Company. By now my leg was swollen and had become very painful. I had four or five chunks of mortar shrapnel in my calf and behind my knee. The corpsman changed my bandage and gave me a shot of morphine in my thigh. In a voice that faltered, he told me that he knew and liked our first sergeant, who was covered in a poncho just a few yards away.

The rest of the night until dawn was like some kind of weird dream. I knew what was going on all right, but I was detached. It was like looking at this event through someone else's eyes. My memories are like many little vignettes: The silhouette of a corpsman pulling a poncho over the head of the dead marine; multiple pyrotechnics swinging down in the background; leaping shadows; the lights, the tracers, the explosions, the screams, and cries of battle. By daylight, it was all over. The NVA had gathered up what dead they could and disappeared into the jungle.

An hour after daylight, I was in a medevac helicopter, headed for triage at the military hospital in Danang. I was there only long enough for a doctor to ask me a couple of questions. Then almost immediately I was loaded back onto another helicopter and flown to a waiting surgical hospital ship, the USS *Repose* (AH16). I woke up when the helicopter landed on the helipad located at the fantail of the ship. I saw a beautiful blue sky and white clouds through the whirling helicopter blades. I saw the blurred faces of sailors looking down from the gang planks above. I heard the sound of an elevator taking me down to the cool interior of the ship, and when I opened my eyes once more in my vision appeared the beautiful face of a navy nurse. She had red freckles, and I could see she had real white teeth when she smiled at me and said, "Hey, Marine. It's going to be okay—we'll have you fixed up good as new in no time." I closed my eyes. I'm okay. They're going to fix me up. I'm okay. I'm okay.

12

I kept hearing a familiar voice calling my name. My eyes opened, but they were not focusing very well. And when they did focus, what I saw made me smile. There was Art Vigil standing next to my bed, eating a Dixie cup full of ice cream.

An RPG had exploded next to him, peppering his head with tiny shards of shrapnel. His whole head was bandaged, like some kind of cheesecloth turban. It was good to see a friendly face, and Art's infectious smile always made me feel a little better. My head was swimming from the anesthesia, as he told me what happened to him—in between mouthfuls of ice cream. I tried even harder to wake up when his story got around to the USS *Repose* having limitless ice cream and pogey bait* in the PX. In between slurping down what was left in the Dixie cup, Art was saying something about nightly movies for enlisted patients out on the helipad and getting my ass out of there because the movie was going to start.

I know I drifted off because when I opened my eyes, there was Art; he had a wheelchair parked next to my bed and was adjusting some pillows on a crutch to prop up my leg. There was a large door on each end of the ward leading to a wide corridor, which led toward the center of the ship. While the corpsmen were busy at the front of the ward, Art loaded me into the wheelchair and snuck me out the back. I kept drifting in and out as Art pushed me down a long hallway deep inside the ship. I woke up when Art handed me a Dixie cup full of ice cream. It was as if I had never eaten ice cream. It tasted so different, so delicious; like something made in heaven. I shoveled in mouth-watering slow-motion spoonfuls as Art flew down the corridor toward the bank of elevators. Eating became too strenuous while waiting for the elevator, and I drifted off again. It was all I

---

* Sweets: candy, ice cream, drinks, etc.

could do to get that spoonful up to my mouth and I dropped my ice cream on the deck as Art rolled me into an elevator. Unlike most naval vessels, hospital ships have elevators and a few stairways instead of ladders. Once the silver doors rolled opened, and the sea air flooded my lungs, my head started to clear quite rapidly.

The fantail was packed with marines wearing blue and white pinstripe bathrobes. Some were in wheelchairs, most had obvious bandages or casts. All of them had had a turn at the ice cream machine, and damn, I dropped mine. The excitation was running high. Scuttlebutt had it that the movie was in Technicolor, and they had three speakers—two in front and one in the back, really cool! The movie turned out to be *Born Free*, a smarmy lion movie shot on some game farm in Africa. It would've been the perfect movie if you were on a date in junior high, but not for a bunch of combat marines. Give us John Wayne, James Bond, even a terrible movie with hot chicks in swimsuits.

Fifteen minutes into the movie, every time the music swelled with the *Born Free* theme, loud booing and catcalls rippled through the audience of disappointed patients. At first I thought it was the rowdy audience that caused the movie to stop and the lights to come up. But I was wrong—there was a ship-wide search going on for me. When my name was called out and I responded, a flock of corpsmen swooped down on me like hungry seagulls—highly pissed, hungry seagulls. When they wheeled me back to the ward, they wanted to know the name of the marine who snuck me off. I told them that I was too groggy and couldn't remember. This little incident pissed off some of the upper echelon hospital squids; they really wanted to bust the marine who had rolled me out of the ward. There is an old saying in the navy and the Marine Corps that "the shit rolls downhill." I know the two corpsmen in charge of the ward got a thorough ass chewing and in turn made the rest of my time in their care as rough as they could. I figured what the hell, what's the worst that they can do to me—sew me up and send me back to Vietnam?

USS Repose
March 14, 1967

Hi Y'all,

Crookston* sent my Purple Heart to you yesterday. Also, I sent a $30 check. Today I signed for another $150 check and I'll mail that home at the end of the month.** I'm going nuts on this ship with all these dippy squids*** running around. I wish I was in Okinawa with the rest of the battalion. Oh well, this ship sails to Subic Bay the 10th of next month. I heard the Philippine Islands were pretty good for liberty. How was it when you were there, Dad? I spent yesterday in the sun convalescing. Paul, here's a thought to ponder. I will spend 13 months sweating, humping miles, carrying tons, sleeping in the mud, eating C rations and getting shot at during my tour, while the closest a squid comes to land is five miles offshore. Don't be an ass-join anything but the crotch****-ha. As to date, I have not received any letters. Oh well, keep writing-I am bound to get them soon. How do you like my picture with the general? Pretty cool, huh? And he knowing Uncle Dick***** made it even better. General Walt is my commanding general.******

I walked a few steps on my sore leg today. It is quite weak still. But soon I will be giving it hell trying to get it back into shape.

(Dad only-) From the reports I get Marines are still fighting very hard in the same area, and every day more Marines are brought in. Dad, that is the same area we were heli-lifted in about a month and a half ago, with the CBS and ABC cameraman, remember? Then we didn't find much but empty bunkers. See how much good that truce did? They just got some damn good Marines killed. The NV A take advantage of this truce bull shit by making mass troop movements, and getting resupplied from China. Every gook we killed in that area had a brand-new AK-47 from China. I am very much against these truces. The Christmas truce caused a damn good squad leader to get killed the day after Christmas. Dad, this is no way to fight a war. It is time we stopped playing around fighting a defensive war. Instead we should sweep through and wipe out every gook in sight . . .

Love

John

---

*   He carried the M-60 machine gun in 2nd Squad
**   There wasn't anywhere to spend money there; I was saving for college
*** Marines' term for sailors
**** Crotch, derogatory term at the time for the Marine Corps.
***** Col. R. C. Nutting USMC Ret.
****** General Walt presented my Purple Heart at my bedside, and mentioned serving with my Uncle Dick in World War II, and spoke very highly of him as a man and a marine

As soon as I was able to get around on crutches, I spent much of my time on the fantail smoking cigarettes in the sunshine, with about eight or ten of the same guys. Most of us had spent that night pinned down by heavy fire. Most of us had heard the marines who were cut off from help, being tortured and killed. Every day on my way out to the fresh air, I would go past wards filled with young marines horrifically wounded. Every day, the helicopters would unload new wounded just in from some battlefield. The same look on the same faces.

The meeting spot on the back of the ship was a great place to get away from what was going on inside. Art Vigil usually had us laughing over his interpretation of any incident—it didn't matter what it was, he could make it funny. Of the group on the fantail, I remember only faces and not their names, and some not at all. I think this is where I first met Lance Corporal Tom Burkhardt. In the following months, Burkhardt and I spent many a night standing watch together. In our storytelling to keep each other awake, we discovered we had an uncanny number of similarities: names and dates, even the same 1961 Ford car, although mine had the Hearst Mystery Shifter. We used to joke with each other, "Keep my ass covered. Because if I get hit, you know you're next."

Sometimes back there on the fantail, the war seemed so far away, almost like we were high school friends sitting in the sunshine, smoking, joking, and telling stories. Vigil wound up his daily version of the world according to Art, there were comments on girlfriends and families, and usually another R&R story about a double-jointed bar girl. Eventually the conversation would always turn to a more serious nature.

The volume of the voices dropped, and the words thinned way out, when the subject got around to us inflicting as much payback as possible on the North Vietnamese Army. One afternoon, I mentioned to the group what our company commander had told me just before we were to go to Okinawa that they were still taking volunteers for 3rd Marine Regimental Scout/Snipers back at Camp Carroll. Anyone who shot expert was eligible, and that I was considering it now, more than ever. Once we started talking about it, we were soon all caught up in the bravado. Snipers usually had it a little better than a line grunt. Most of the time they didn't have to stand watch at night and were able to operate somewhat independently in the field. Usually when a grunt company got hit, the odds were in the NVA's favor. Being a much smaller and quieter target seemed to give a sniper a little more control over his ultimate fate in Vietnam. In joining the snipers, we would be able to go back to Camp Carroll—an area we were familiar with—and hopefully be able to "inflict as much pain and suffering as possible" on the NVA, who had caused so much pain and suffering to our brothers and fellow marines.

13

After making the decision to join the snipers, I was highly motivated to get off *Repose*. I pushed hard in physical therapy, and a few days after my stitches were out, I found myself back at Camp Carroll. The sniper tents were located in the same area of the plateau that I was headquartered in with the grunts. It was like being back in the old neighborhood, only I had moved up from across the tracks. The sniper tents had high sandbag walls around them and were located on slightly elevated ground, back away from the lines. Snipers also had a couple of real nice bunkers with thick, reinforced sandbag ceilings. The cherry on top was I had a tent with my own cot and a foot locker—real first-class accommodations for Camp Carroll,

Settling in to snipers wasn't too hard since there were a lot of familiar faces and every few days or so, *Repose* would release one of the guys from our old grunt outfit.

I don't remember any formal training about what we had to do as a sniper or any classes to help us think like snipers. However, we were allowed as much target practice as we had time for.

It was during one of my first target practices that I was given some old sage advice from Corporal Joe Ciscineros, a sniper who was going home in a couple of weeks. He said, "Remember, Nutting, as a sniper, your mantra is 'one shot; one kill.' Make every one count." We were all grunts, we all shot expert, and we all had seen combat. I knew enough to use natural camouflage and face paint when necessary, but I never heard the term "ghillie suit" until I was out of the Marine Corps. Corporal Joe was a short handsome Mexican with a big, white-toothed smile and an easy-going nature. He was a solid sniper in the field and well liked by all of us. He was one of the few married snipers; I had seen a picture of his wife. A couple weeks after Corporal Joe rotated back into the world, word came down that he had been shot and killed by his wife's new boyfriend.

I remember being extremely impressed by the quality of the rifle I was issued and how accurately it fired. I spent the next two weeks firing countless rounds, getting to "know" my Remington 700, with a floating barrel and its Redfield 3x9 scope, "better than your girlfriend back home," We fired 7.62 mm match ammunition. I was stoked. What a job—unlimited target practice with free ammunition. The Remington 700 was the finest rifle I had ever shot. Learning how to use a scope took a little getting used to, but soon snuggling my cheek into the stock was as comfortable as dancing cheek-to-cheek at Peg's Teen Inn.

It didn't take me long to notice that the morale in the scout/sniper platoon was very low. Our job as scout/snipers was to be deployed with the grunt companies within the regiment on large-scale operations or even short patrols. Gunnery Sergeant Costello was in charge of snipers, and it was said he had spent most of his tour in his sandbag bunker. Most of the dissension had occurred during lulls in combat, when snipers weren't required in the field. Gunny Costello would become twitchy with so many undeployed sniper teams on the plateau. Costello started sniper patrols, which went badly from the start. Too many people, too easily spotted, very little firepower, and little consideration for the terrain, were some of the reasons I remember sniper patrols weren't more successful. There was a jar stuffed with money MPC* that grew larger every payday that would be collected by the Marine who put a cap in Costello. The word was also out that Swede** was very serious about collecting the cash.

Not long after I joined snipers, word came down that Gunny Costello knew about the contract on him, and it had worried him so much that he had come up with a plan that would change the morale of the entire sniper company. That plan came in the form of Gunnery Sergeant Bobby Merrill, a highly decorated combat veteran from the Korean War. Sergeant Merrill

---

*   Military payment certificates

** Bjorn Dahlin, a.k.a. Swede, is still my friend and brother today. He has written a book called *From Mercenary to Missionary*. In the early 1980s was flown to Sweden by Swedish National Television to appear on a *This Is Your Life*-type of program about Bjorn.

was a short redheaded man who chained-smoked Camel cigarettes and had a perpetually worried look on his face. He once showed me a picture of his new wife, who was from Oceanside, California, and about twenty years his junior. I think he worried a lot about her overall welfare, being so young and alone in a navy town.

Sergeant Merrill's first mission to improve 3rd Marine scout/snipers' morale, unfortunately, was one of Gunny Costello's sniper patrols. The idea looked pretty good on paper. We were to leave Camp Carroll about midnight, work our way across the valley, set up on a steep ridge before dawn, and catch any enemy movement when it became light. Everyone on that patrol was a little extra pumped up—maybe we were going to kick some ass and take some names for a change. We moved almost soundlessly, and we made good time, reaching the ridge—well before dawn—undetected. I was toward the front of our patrol and I had already started to set in on the ridge when all hell broke loose; a FUBAR* patrol for the books had just started.

My old friend Tom Lazich later filled me in on the details. Lazich was behind Sergeant Merrill on the patrol and observed him drinking almost continuously from his canteens, so that by the time he reached the base of the ridge he needed to fill both of his canteens with water from the small creek running along its base. Tom told me later that he did warn Sergeant Merrill that drinking too much water in too short a time would make him sick, and he was told to "shut the fuck up." About the time Sergeant Merrill got halfway up to the ridge, he started vomiting loudly, again and again, the noise echoing off the valley walls, just as it was beginning to get light. I couldn't believe it—anyone within miles around would know where we were now, and to make matters worse, after megaphone-puking the rest of the way up to the ridge, Merrill called a medevac in and had his ass medevaced off the ridge as soon as it got light. Nothing like letting the enemy know where we were, and without the element of surprise and camouflage, we were easy pickings. We had to move, fast.

---

*   Fucked up beyond all recognition

We couldn't return the way we had come, so we had to hack our way through thick mountainous jungle to reach Highway 9. It was a nightmare of slowly hacking through thick brush in stifling heat and inching our way up seemingly vertical hillsides. The NVA were close by although they did not fully attack us—an element dogged us for the next day and a half taking potshots at us, keeping us on the move. In hindsight I think they wanted us out of the area without a major confrontation and without calling attention to a large troop movement.

A little humor came out of all this misery. We had a new sergeant named Johnson. This was his first patrol, and since Merrill had to be medevaced, Johnson was now in charge. Just as it was getting dark, it started pouring heavy rain. We couldn't dig in, so we drew in together on a little knob of ground in the thick bush, backpack to backpack, giving us a 360 degree of protection. There is a lizard in the jungle that the marines call the "fuck you lizard." It call starts off sounding like someone in a very high voice, hysterically laughing and then going "Fuck youuuuuu!"

We told Sergeant Johnson that they were drug-crazed NVAs, who were probably going to attack at any time. Sergeant Johnson probably knew it was all bullshit, but nonetheless he stayed awake during the entire night, while the rest of us were able to nod off in fitful periods of exhaustion, between watches.

By late afternoon the next day we had hacked our way out of the jungle and reached Highway 9 and eventually made it back to Camp Carroll. The stack of MPCs in the contract jar kept growing in size.

14

My Dearest Parents,

Well, I am right back in the old groove again. Getting up at 4:30 a.m. and tromping around in the jungle for three to 10 days. As hard as it is, I like the excitement. Like we found an old abandoned NVA base camp-probably used when they were fighting the French. Bamboo beds, tables-the whole bit. We stopped and ate chow there. As you know, snipers work in pairs. My partner is a big Swede. He fought with United Nations forces in Cyprus, and was a mercenary in the Congo. He's a good guy to have with you in the field. I have trouble understanding him at times because his speech is broken and he gets his words mixed up. Tomorrow I'm going to Dong Ha. They are going to x-ray my leg again. It's sort of bothered me on the long walk. Like the docs said, it is probably just muscle tissue healing. I have decided to go on RR to Taipei at the end of the month. That is Taipei Taiwan. I've got $200 on the books so I should have a good time.

Love,

John

Tuesday, April 9

My Dearest Parents,

I am sorry to say I am back from R&R and I had a wonderful time. My R&R started on the 30th and ended on the 5th. Five days of being a civilian again, and what a blowout. Here I go again, getting ahead of myself. I guess I had better start at the beginning. We got into Taipei at 6 p.m. There were four of us, two Seabees and two Marines, which turned out to be quite a group. We stayed at the new Taipei Hotel. Being hot and dirty after the trip, we decided to shower and hit the town, but when I unlocked my room, guess what I found? A broad. And she thought I was going to show her a good time-Ha! She went out the door so fast she didn't even get to say hello. My partners also had the same experience. They also got rid of their girls. In summary, I did quite a lot of sleeping, eating in the bathtub and drinking. I did meet a girl. She was beautiful of course. I didn't see too many ugly ones. Taipei had some living dolls. Her name was Shomi-and she did. I went to a Buddhist temple in the mountains and did some shopping. . . . my first night or morning when I woke up I didn't know where I was.

Boy, what a change in 24 hours. I changed from a combat Marine to an easy living civilian, in a plush hotel. That's quite a change. . . . Tomorrow I'm going out to Delta five to stay about two to four weeks. It should be pretty fun although I don't like standing watch. I am over halfway through my tour in Nam and I am thinking about extending for overseas duty-maybe in Okinawa or Japan.

Love,
John

Little did I expect what was coming down the pike.

The day we moved out, our destination was the old rat-infested, abandoned French fort, Delta 5. It was northwest of the small village called Thon Dinh Son, about a half a mile down a one-lane dirt road. From there, we were assigned to a newly formed combined action company (CAC) located at the edge of the village and composed of a long, low structure, likely a leftover French administration building. This was surrounded and protected by concertina wire, claymore mines, and thick sandbag walls encircling our compound.

CAC was comprised of troops from the South Vietnamese Army (ARVN) and Marines joined together with sympathetic locals. We would teach the locals how to defend their village, which turned out to be pretty much a farce, since many of the people we were teaching—if they weren't actually NVA—were NVA sympathizers. The rest were simple farmers who were scared to death of what the NVA would do to them and would never fight them anyway.

The payoff was that you didn't have to go on operations for weeks at a time; you're in this compound shared by ARVN running small patrols out and around the village, making the CAC presence known. At nighttime the NVA would come in to the village and get supplies, get laid, and terrorize the civilian population.

However, I also was developing appreciation for the country. I thought Vietnam was beautiful. I liked being around the Vietnamese people, and I liked their customs. I thought that being in the CAC unit was a wonderful opportunity. Many of the snipers thought that being in the CAC had your "ass way too far out in front of the wire." It was a dangerous place, but most of Vietnam was a dangerous place, and unlike Camp Carroll, the village was beautiful. The main building we were living in must've been built by the French; it was a miniature fortress on the outskirts of a picturesque village settled in this lush green valley, with the Camp Carroll Plateau on one side and the jungle-covered mountains on the other.

[no date]

Dear Mom and Dad,

In my last letter I told you I was moving to Delta Five. It didn't happen, instead six sniper teams moved to C.A.C. the latter is where we live in a village with the people, guard them while they work, then run patrols at night. I enjoy the work and it is far from routine. We have to watch our manners. It is very easy to insult these people without knowing it. When invited to dinner, which is an honor, you must take a portion of everything that is served, and eat it. I never thought I would be eating fish heads and rice topped with some sort of sauce, but I did. When I left I looked more or less like the country-Green. Another drawback is the NVA infiltrators coming into the village at night in search for food and supplies. We got one last night. Despite our efforts there are a lot of sympathizers. I have a little buddy who is about Paul's age. I call him "Fly." The reason is, I can't get rid of him. Everywhere I go, he is right behind me. He is my interpreter and I am beginning to pick up some of the language. I got a new job, which is I make up the patrol routes to take the squad out and set up ambush sites. I think it is a lot of fun.

Love,

John

Thon Dinh Son had a small marketplace in the village center. Occasionally I would go into the village and get a haircut or buy some unroasted peanuts and drink a warm Vietnamese beer. I don't know when I first started carrying the corpsman bag when I went into the village. It's one of those things that just happened. Soon, every time I went to buy some peanuts, I had an increasingly large crowd crying "Bac Si, Bac Si, (Dr.) you number one, you fix, you fix." I "fix" splinters, cuts, infections, jungle rot, sprains, headaches, and cramps. A clean dressing worked wonders. The villagers loved iodine on small cuts and abrasions; the more it burned, the better the medicine.

There was a mustang lieutenant in charge of CAC. He liked me, and he supported us going into the village with "hearts and minds" intentions. He did get upset when he heard that I once went into the village unarmed, but I explained to him that the one time I did it, I was trying to make a statement and that I never went into the village without Art or Bjorn—or both—and their trusty M-16s. One time, the corpsman and I were able to get a Vietnamese woman with a breach pregnancy medevaced out of the village. She had been in labor many hours. There had been some bullshit about using government property to medevac "civilian gooks." This was about the time our government started trying to win "hearts and minds." After some passionate haranguing, and threats of "taking this all the way to the top," we were granted a medevac all the way to Danang. It turned out well; the mother and baby were okay, and at the time I felt we really did win a few villagers' hearts and minds.

May 16

Dearest Folks,

It's six o'clock and the sun is going down after a real scorcher. I'm sitting by my bunker and writing and watching the people. I'll describe what I see. On the left is a man with his little boy plowing a plot of ground. His plow is crudely made out of wood. His little boy has a stick popping the stubborn water buffalo. A little right of that is the Catholic Church with numerous grass huts behind it. In front of me is a very small woman with her little boy. It looks as if they were picking peanuts. Two young boys to my left are bringing the cows in from a pasture at the village edge. Notice all are either pre-teen or old people, the rest are in the army, either North or South. Something that amazes me-everyone works all the time and they work very hard. Little girls about eight or nine, carrying 40 pound bundles; boys Paul's age, doing a man's work. Something that has been in the back of my mind is that

I would like to come back here when I'm out of the Marine Corps, maybe with the Peace Corps and work in this country, or one like it. I got the pictures today, and I sort of had that old familiar lump in my throat. I can't believe how the kids are growing up (Vikki looks much older and Chris-I just don't believe it). Dad—that's a mighty classy looking sweater—whoever bought it must have good taste. I hope I don't have to rotate back to the Plateau, I'm having fun here; looks like it's going to rain in about 30 minutes, I wish I had some good books to read.

Love,
John

It was like a little paradise down in Thon Din Son. Most of the time we were running routine patrols, teaching the Vietnamese forces fire team tactics, how to set up an effective ambush, and generally how to protect their village. For the most part we settled into a very comfortable routine with very little combat.

There are many human-interest stories from that time. One in particular touched my heart in an unexpected way: one night we set an ambush up on the edge of town. Nothing happened during the night, and just before light we began to move out back to the compound. Our corpsman had gone to sleep, and we unknowingly left him behind.

He awoke with a start to find all of us gone and an NVA creeping past him just a few feet away. He carried a double-barreled, sawed-off shotgun with fleshette rounds. This is a shotgun shell packed with many one-inch metal darts. He fired both rounds into the NVA. This soldier turned out to be the son of the village's top man, and an NVA, who was sneaking back home for supplies. I'm not sure who gave the order, but by command, his body was pulled into the village center and left there all day in the hot sun for everyone to see what had happened to him. I saw the pain this caused his father. There was nothing he could do until the sun went down, when he could take his son home to bury him.

15

Our patrol the next day started out like any other; it seemed so at first, anyway. We left the compound early in the morning while it was still cool. In hindsight that was about the only thing comparable about this patrol. One difference was I was carrying the corpsman's bag; I'd never carried the corpsman's bag on a patrol before. Our corpsman had to go up to the plateau to pick up a shipment of inoculations for the village. We were excited that they okayed our shipment. This was our "hearts and minds" project for this village.

Since I was the corpsman on this patrol, my position was second behind the radioman or sixth in line. There were probably three or four more behind me. Art Vigil and Tom Burkhardt (my doppelganger) ran point—as number one and number two. There were no ARVN with us on this patrol, but I don't remember why.

Nelson had just made corporal, and this was his first time leading a patrol. He was just ahead of me. It was a beautiful day, late morning and not too hot, when we took a smoke break next to the cemetery at the edge of the village. Across the road was a large rice paddy with about a dozen people working in it. I had barely pulled off my pack and lit a cigarette, when the villagers came out of the rice paddy. It seemed that about half of them gathered around me, saying "hey, *Boc Si, Boc Si,* you number one, you number one" while showing me a cut or a sore. Being able to give aid in that way gave me a great deal of satisfactiossn.

In less than fifteen minutes we loaded up and got ready to move out. In hindsight, it was strange that no one noticed or became suspicious that the villagers didn't go back into the rice paddy; instead they headed back down the trail toward the village.

The trail we were taking away from the village took a sharp turn around the edge of the cemetery between the rice paddies. I barely started around the edge of the dogleg when there were two simultaneous explosions. I was diving for cover before I even had time to think, but I do remember vividly seeing a human leg with a jungle boot on it helicoptering over my head while I was still in the air.

Like a bad movie, I remember some events in kind of a distorted slow motion. I knew Art and Tom had to be in trouble as I raced forward through the smoke and dust. Tom was lying on his back on the trail. He was intact but he wasn't moving. His face was covered in red dirt when I started CPR on him. Pink foam started bubbling out of his chest. I don't know how long I tried to get Tom to come back before I became aware of cries of "corpsman up, corpsman up" and I realized then that I was the corpsman.

"Oh my God, I *am* the corpsman!" I told the dead marine, my friend and brother with whom I had so many similarities, and vowed to cover his ass, that I was sorry, but I had to go.

I got up and started running back down the trail. Almost immediately I saw out of the corner of my eye something off in the ditch. Something happened in that split second: I knew what I saw was a skull missing its jaw bone. And there were some ribs, and I knew it was Art. At the same time I heard this voice telling me I couldn't stop, and I couldn't look, and I stepped out of the slow-motion trance to multiple loud cries of "corpsman up, corpsman up." Everyone was wounded except me. Everyone had caught a lot of shrapnel.

The radioman had a sucking chest wound that I managed to plug up with several cellophane wrappers from the C rations cigarette packages. Nelson had a bad leg wound and was in a lot of pain. His femoral artery was nicked. I had a hard time controlling his bleeding.

One marine named Zider was able to call in the medevacs. He was hit with a piece of shrapnel about the size of a large pea, next to his kneecap. While Zider helped the wounded onto the medevacs, I took a poncho and went to look for the pieces of my friend Art Vigil. I think I went into slow motion again. When Art ran point, he usually carried several fragmentation grenades on his belt. He was probably standing directly on top of a hand detonated artillery shell booby trap. The concussion set off the grenades on his belt.

I have this nightmare memory of feeling the need to find all of his parts to send home. The pilots and the door gunner in the medevac helicopter were having a panic attack; they get real nervous sitting on the ground. When I started looking, there were parts of Art all over.

When I had collected all that I could find and I started dragging my poncho to the waiting helicopter, I realized that parts of Art had been sliding out of the poncho's head opening, and I had to go back and pick up these parts using my helmet to returning them to the rest of Art on the poncho at the helicopter. On this final trip, my eyes locked with the door gunner as he helped me load Art into the helicopter. In that instant our glances spoke volumes.

Although wounded, Zider declined to be medevaced; he didn't want his wound to be reported. His mother was dying of cancer, and if you get wounded, they send a telegram home saying your son has been wounded in action, et cetera. I know we both experienced a "What the fuck!" moment when the medevac disappeared, everything became quiet again, and it was just the two of us alive out there. It seemed like an eternity, but probably was only fifteen minutes, before we heard the comforting roar of a tank coming for us.

Fortunately for Zider and me; this wasn't a full-scale ambush. This was one guy hiding in the bush waiting to pull the cord, and before I got to my feet after the explosion, he had long disappeared into the undergrowth.

What I remember of the ride back to the compound is that it seemed like the tank took forever—a slow-motion green blur. I didn't look any more, and I couldn't really feel myself.

16

I could hardly breathe. It may have been the oppressive late-afternoon heat or the red dust churned up by the tanks, but by the time the tank dropped Zider and me off at the front gate of CAC, I had a tightness in my chest like I was squeezing off a deep cut and I couldn't let go to see how bad it was.

All the while that I was working to remove the small piece of shrapnel from next to Zider's kneecap, a darkness was snowballing inside me. By the time I put the last bit of tape on Zider's dressing, it was seeping around the edges, and my chest was filling up. I had never felt such anger, rage, hatred, or sense of betrayal. Every villager in the rice paddy that day knew the NVA soldier was hiding in the bush, waiting to detonate his booby trap.

I thought I had established at least a friendly relationship with five or six of the people who came to me that day by the cemetery. I felt that if they had only told me, hinted, given me some kind of sign, anything, while I was dabbing on some iodine or handing out a cigarette, Tom and Art would still be alive.

Payback is a motherfucker, and I was going to hand out some payback, big time. Those who I knew personally, who smiled and looked into my eyes and said nothing, were going to pay with their lives. I filled up several extra magazines for my M-16, stepped out of the compound door into the low, late afternoon sunshine, and headed for the compound's front gate.

With everything else going on, I'd tried to ignore the ever-increasing sharp intestinal cramps. There was no getting around it. Before anything else happened, I had to use the shitter. The atmosphere in our shitter in the late afternoon became that of a very hot and humid sauna, and smelled like melting turds. I know I wanted to get out of there as fast as I could. I tried to hold my breath as long as possible. I reached in my utility trouser pocket for my C rations roll of toilet paper and pulled out a single dose of inject-able morphine. I think they were called a syrette and came two to a pack.

This was the one I hadn't used when I injected Nelson, when he was in a lot of pain not only from his wound but from seeing how badly his first patrol went. The next thing I remember is seeing the syrette stuck in my bare thigh. I don't remember doing it. I've thought about it many times. In my mind I can see the toilet paper roll and a syringe of morphine in my hand. I don't remember sticking it in my thigh. I do remember feeling like I slowly started to collapse in on myself, mentally and emotionally *and* spiritually. I don't think you can call it crying; it was something else. I don't think I made much noise.

Afterward, nobody let on if they heard me. If there is such a thing, it was like a spiritual vomiting. I had so much grief and disappointment, and yet I had been taught long ago that before I make judgments on other people, to put myself in their shoes.

In my heart of hearts, I knew that had I been one of those Vietnamese farmers, especially the three I knew personally, I would not have jeopardized my welfare or the lives of my family by informing on the NVA soldier and his booby trap. When I think about that time, it is like a nightmare of jumbled thoughts and emotions so extreme that even after so many years it is difficult and painful to think about, let alone form into words.

I think the morphine put a tourniquet on my spiritual hemorrhage just in time. I can only say that I stayed in that fetid oven and vented my rage at my maker and life itself until the putrid darkness drained away from me into the shitter.

Sometime later, when I opened the shitter door and walked into the fresh air, I looked the same on the outside, but inside I was different.

The worm had turned for me.

Captured NVA weapons: mortars, rockets, bouncing Bettys, C-4 plastic explosive. Photo courtesy Steven Stafford.

Vietnamese children in the village. Few adults except elderly were ever present. Photo courtesy Steven Stafford.

Typical view of rice paddy in the foreground with a village in tree-line background. Photo courtesy Steven Stafford.

Chinook helicopter delivering supplies and mail. Ammunition was also delivered in this manner. Photo courtesy Steven Stafford.

Front row, left to right: J. J. Rhodes, Art Vigil (center), John Nutting waiting for USO show to begin at Camp Carroll. Photo from the author's collection.

Author with Mom and Kristine on the day he left for staging at Camp Pendleton on his way to Vietnam. Photo from the author's collection.

Marines cleaning serving trays and cooking pots behind mess hall at Camp Carroll. The infamous rock-filled grease and rat-filled pit is on far lower left. Photo from the author's collection.

Author, as a marine sniper, with Remington 700 rifle and 3x9 Redfield scope. Photo from the author's collection.

Author writing a letter home. Photo from the author's collection.

Sniper team Dahlin and Nutting applying camouflage to each other before heading out to a sniper post. Photo from the author's collection.

A very unhappy Mae on the day the author left Bangkok, returning to Vietnam. Photo from the author's collection.

From left, standing: Bjorn Dahlin, (note knife strapped to leg that became a legacy); J. J. Johnson, checking tattoo; Art Vigil in background (later killed in action); Gerald Aylor with pencil and an aspiring writer (also, later killed in action); Nutting wearing hat; Berke with glasses (came to snipers from hospital ship); and Nelson (who later fatefully lead the patrol when the Combined Action Company patrol was ambushed). Kneeling left front: David Schroy (loved and missed his car most of all). Kneeling right front: Corporal Joe Ciscineros (shot and killed by wife's new boyfriend a few days after arriving home). Photo courtesy Charlie Keyes.

Author with "short timer's hat and stick." Two items traditionally passed on to the departing Marine on his last day at Camp Carroll. Photo from the author's collection.

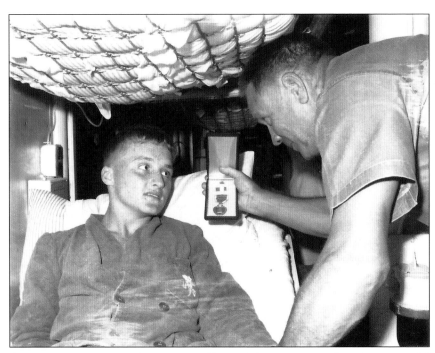

Author in his hospital bed aboard the naval hospital ship, *USS Repose*. He is being awarded the Purple Heart by Marine Corps General Lewis William Walt. General Walt served in World War II with and was a friend to John Nutting's uncle Colonel Richard Nutting.

Propaganda leaflets were dropped from aircraft by the thousands on trails and areas known to be inhabited by the VC and NVA. These leaflets appeared to be prized more by the enemy for their use as toilet paper. Photo from the author's collection.

Envelope from the front lines covered with Vietnamese red mud.
Mail from combat zones was free. Envelopes were so marked. Photo
from the author's collection.

Front and back of a postcard sent to my parents using the label from
the case of 7.62 Match ammunition (sniper bullets). The only writing
materials I had at the time. Photo from the author's collection.

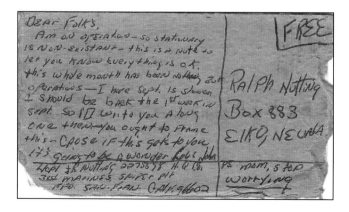

17

About a minute after the evening curfew was in effect, our lieutenant called in artillery in a huge fire mission in the free fire zone. It seemed like most of the 105s and 155s at Camp Carroll opened up. Maybe it was extra big to boost our morale. With so many wounded and the deaths of Art and Tom we were all feeling our own sense of loss and pain.

I stayed out of the village; I stood a lot of watches so I could be by myself. I went on two-man ambush patrols with Swede. I read everything that I could find and I wrote many letters. And a few times I smoked some pot. Like any other time I smoked pot in Vietnam, it was never in the field, most of the time in a bunker, and never on watch.

A bunker was a four-foot-wide L- or T-shaped trench with a thick sandbag roof. Usually it was pitch black inside, with two to ten guys and this little red glow being passed around. Just voices in the darkness, talking about girlfriends, cars, great stories from past lives. So many times it seemed like the sanest thing going on in my life—this little pitch-black safety zone of muffled sounds and reefer smoke.

A couple of days after Tom and Art died, a sniper—I can't remember who—invited me into the bunker. He had just returned from R&R, and he had heard the bad news. I think he wanted to cheer me up, and he told me he had "a real treat" from Bangkok, Thailand. "Park Lanes" look like a regular pack of filter-tipped cigarettes with a turquoise outer wrapper and a pink bull's-eye—kind of like a Lucky Strikes package. However, they were filled with high-grade Thai marijuana. The Park Lane was no doubt the very best reefer I had ever smoked, but it was more memorable for how it felt like an ointment for the pain I was feeling inside. Not like the morphine I had injected into my leg four days before—that had truly diverted a personal disaster.

A little side memory of that time was when I walked out of the bunker—higher than I had ever been in my life—and headed for the pisser,

I saw the lieutenant walking straight toward me. I had no alternative but to continue walking straight toward him, eye contact all the way, and give him a nod of recognition (no salute in a combat zone). I know I must've smelled like a field of burned hay, and my eyeballs felt like they had varicose veins. I thought then my goose was really cooked, but we just walked past each other. He avoided the bunker altogether. He was a mustang lieutenant who came up from the ranks. I liked and respected him. I wish I could remember his name.

A couple of weeks after Art and Tom were killed, I wrote a letter to my dad asking him to write a letter to his senator or congressman, requesting that 3rd Marine scout/snipers get Starlight scopes—"the right equipment for the job we needed to do." He was the Chamber of Commerce manager in Elko, Nevada, at the time, and I thought he might have some clout. I told him I had read in *Stars and Stripes* that the army had the new Starlight scopes, and according to the article in the newspaper, the army snipers were racking up a large number of enemies killed in the short time since they were issued. I wondered why the Marines didn't have those Starlight scopes.

June 15, 1967
Walter S. Bearing, Congressman
Old House Office Building
Washington, DC

Dear Congressman Bearing,

The following comes from two separate letters received recently form [*sic*] my son, PFC John R. Nutting, 3rd Marine Scout Sniper Platoon. I might add that John was wounded February 28 and has been back in action for over two months. He had over 60 stitches in his right leg as a result of an enemy mortar fire. It happened where the so-called truce gave the VC a chance to have all the approaches zeroed in. I believe the following bears out some of the comments in your latest election regarding Mr. McNamara.

Dear Dad,

Something has to be done now. Too many of my friends have been killed because of the lack of equipment and being employed wrong. I wish you would write to your congressman and tell him of this problem; also is it possible to bring it up at some of the business meetings. In CAC* at night snipers are practically helpless as it stands now. We have a regular scope, which is only good in the daytime.

The VC are coming into the village at night taking food and medicine and killing people etc. what we need is a Starlight scope, which will enable us to see at night and to get the kills we need. The Starlight scope doesn't need heavy batteries and a lot of gear. Also it can be detached. I can't explain how important these scopes are, especially during the summer push. Dad, the men here are more than willing to give their lives for their country. Why won't the people of the US give us their cooperation and help us with the equipment we need? Granted, the Starlight scopes are very expensive, but what is the cost of a US Marines life? I wish you would get someone on this, and see why the 3rd Marine snipers can't get the scopes.

Dad, I am tired of seeing my friends killed when there is no visible end to this war. I would rather die storming Hanoi than watching my buddies be picked off one by one. Most of my buddies feel the same way. I would like to hear America tell Hanoi, either stop right now, or we will blow the hell out of you, and then do it. As things are going now this could go on for a hundred years. I am not a warmonger, but even if we clear Vietnam, there is Laos and Cambodia. Ho Chi Minh knows this and that is why he doesn't want peace talks. I say blow the [blanked out] out of his sanctuary now, and he'll be begging for peace talks, I wish they would turn us loose and let us fight hard for a year. I hate to think of Paul having to get into this.

Dad, you know as well as I do-you can't explain a combat situation to someone who has never taken part in it. I wish something could be done. Today is Buddha's birthday. The village is being decorated and they will roast a pig for the celebration tonight. The more I work with these people as a corpsman, the more I see the need for modernization and sanitation. This would be an ideal place for the Peace Corps when this is over. I would like to be a part of it when I get out. I think it would be very rewarding work. Do you realize I graduated from high school a year ago tomorrow? In lots of ways it seems much longer than that and then again it seems only like it was yesterday.

---

*   Combined Action Company

[Conclusion of my father's letter]

As John's father, Mr. Bearing, and speaking for the other parents, these boys have a marvelous ability to boost their own morale if they feel we are behind them. Let's give them the equipment for the job and the go ahead to get this thing over and so they can come back, and get their educations and become the kind of citizens they wish to be.

Mr. Bearing, I appreciate a great many of your political views and particularly agree with you on your military views. Naturally, I wonder just what your reaction to this letter will be.

Sincerely,

Ralph Nutting

Walter S. Bearing
Congress of the United States
House of Representatives,
Washington, DC.
June 21, 1967
Mr. Ralph Nutting P.O. Box 883
Elko Nevada

Dear Mr. Nutting,

Thank you so much for your letter of June 15, which contained two letters from your son. I've taken the liberty of making a copy of your letter and I am sending it to the Chairman of the Armed Services Committee to see if some action can be taken right away to get the much-needed Starlight scope to the 3rd Marine snipers. With the billions of dollars we are spending daily on the war, there is no excuse for your son and his comrades not to have the Starlight scope or any other equipment that they need. Your son's life and those of all our boys in Vietnam is worth a lot more to me than the cost of any piece of equipment.

As I mentioned above, I am bringing this matter to the attention of Congressman Mendel Rivers, who is the Chairman of the Armed Services Committee, urging that he review this situation.

Letter number two from your son touched me deeply. I read and reread many times the sentence "I would rather die storming Hanoi than watch my buddies be picked off one by one." I well understand his feeling of the futility of it all. I too have that feeling when I see the president listening to such an inexperienced military man as McNamara on how to win the war. It seems like sheer folly. I pray that God will look over your son and see that he returns home to fulfill his ambition. I would like your permission and that of your son, John to print his letter in the Congressional record so that other members of the Congress can be as proud of your son as I am. With every good wish, I am

Sincerely,

Walter S. Bearing

Congressman for Nevada

Every day I was getting more frustrated being in a Combined Action Company, and I just had to get out. I didn't want to go into the village anymore or carry the first aid pack. I put in for a transfer back up to Camp Carroll. But while waiting for transfer orders, I went on several ambushes with Bjorn and never got a shot. I wanted so badly to spot someone setting booby traps. I ached for some kind of revenge, but it never happened. The most memorable thing that did happen was the last time Bjorn and I went out on our "killer team."

Bjorn and I had set up an ambush on a small hill overlooking several trails that intersected around the end of a large rice paddy. We were in position way before dawn, hoping to catch an NVA going or coming from the village, just at light. Now it was well past dawn, and it was already starting to get hot. More and more farmers were coming to work in the rice paddy. It was time to pack up and slip away unnoticed. About the same time, I spotted through my field binoculars what appeared to be a farmer moving toward the edge of the rice paddy. He was coming our way. He had the usual dress of a peasant, the conical straw hat and black "pajamas." What drew my suspicion was the odd way he was moving. He shuffled along with an unusual stooped posture and an erratic gait. His arms and hands were in front of him like he was holding something or trying to hide something under his shirt.

This could be the guy. I called Bjorn's attention to him, and he quickly picked the target up in his scope. I heard Bjorn click off the safety. I saw the sweat beading up on his forehead; the sun was starting to shine right on us. The sweat was starting to run into my eyes as I focused with my binoculars. As the spotter, besides calling in the shot, I had to verify that this truly was an enemy with some kind of weapon or booby trap. Between Bjorn and me, hidden in the elephant grass on the side of the small hill was a patch of dense brush at the edge of the rice paddy. Things became tense as I lost sight of the target as he got close to the brush. I suspect this was where he was hiding his booby trap. We got him! Seconds later he came into view on the front side of the brush. I felt my heart pick up speed. *Praise be to Chesty,* can it get any better than this? Finally, we'll nail this little bastard. Give us anything, just a tiny glimpse of your AK-47 and the big Swede is going to ding one right between your running lights.*

Both Bjorn and I continued to watch the farmer under high magnification. He took another quick furtive look around, moved back toward the brush, with his back toward us, dropped his pants, squatted, and blew out a long stream of diarrhea. It was just a farmer who ate some bad fish or something—and it probably gave him severe cramps, so his movements appeared suspicious, and for *this* he almost got shot.

Bjorn and I just looked at each other and without saying anything, we disappeared into the bush. We were within a breath away from killing an innocent man. At least he was innocent for that instant. He still could been our guy. He could have been the top NVA guy in the area—with the shits. Vietnam was like that. *Fuck this place, fuck CAC; I have to get out of here.*

---

* Chesty Puller is one of the most, if not the most, decorated members of the Marine Corps in its history

18

After transferring from CAC, I was in the field most of the summer months. I found that I preferred spotting over shooting. On two- or four-man teams, I liked the scouting part most of all. I had learned to read a map and use a compass in Boy Scouts, and by now, I was becoming very familiar with much of our area, step-by-step. I would come back to Camp Carroll for a day or two for some hot chow and some quality rack time on a genuine cot before being called in on another operation. Things were heating up not only in enemy contact; the temperature was beginning to feel just as deadly.

Day after day, in the relentless heat, climbing steep terrain, wearing a cumbersome flak jacket and helmet, plus packing my field gear all started to wear me down physically and mentally. So many times I saw a marine loaded up into a body bag and helicoptered out, and I would think, "Fuck, man, I do not want to die here; I don't want to go home like that." I remember more than once having the unsettling feeling of watching a medevac disappear over the tree line, sorry for the guys in the bags and feeling so grateful that it wasn't me.

During one of those once anticipated and all too brief periods back at Camp Carroll, I had a chance encounter I think about occasionally. Around mid-August, the duty of standing watch down on the perimeter came to the snipers. A series of bunkers tucked behind layers of claymore mines and concertina razor wire surrounded the entire perimeter of Camp Carroll. The bunkers down in front of the snipers were dry and well-built with thick sandbag roofs and large enough to accommodate two occupants comfortably.

Late one afternoon just at the sun was about the set, I was sitting on the roof of a bunker having one last cigarette while it was still light. Corporal J. J. Rhodes—the marine who shared guard duty with me that day came down the line and joined me. I had not met him until that day—but I heard many stories about the legacy he had left in Vietnam on a previous tour before rotating back to the United States. That had been before I joined snipers. It seemed liked most of the old salts in snipers had a story about Corporal Rhodes, although no one seemed to agree about how many kills he had on his record or how many times he shot a gook or slit his throat in front of his fellow prisoners "to get the rest jabbering like a bunch of jabbering fucking monkeys."

Did he really jump up on several occasions screaming "you mother-fuckers" when he came under fire, spraying bullets when he disappeared into the bush only to return later with "a couple of ears and a big grin"? Most every old salt claimed to have seen his collection of ears—one for each verified kill. I never saw dried-up ears around his neck or a bloody upside-down cross painted on his forehead as rumors held. However, I did see an upside-down cross shaved in the hair on his chest, and all his web gear and his utility jacket had an upside-down cross drawn on it with a permanent marker.

Rhodes sat on the bunker, and we got acquainted in the few minutes of tropical twilight. Eventually, I got around to asking Rhodes how he managed to be back here in 3rd Marine snipers after he rotated back to the world. He told me that when he first returned home to the old neighbor-hood, he threw himself a welcome home party. From his description, this was a real first-class affair complete with a real live band and catered food. No one showed up except for his girlfriend and a couple old buddies off the block. It seemed like he had become like a pariah, and nobody wanted to be around him. He couldn't sleep. He said he became afraid of night-mares, "almost as real as life itself." He drank every day until he passed out and fell off the barstool. We both laughed when he told me about being in a bar and "still sober enough" to stand up and punch out a couple of hippies. They had cut the American flag in pieces and were wearing them as patches on bell-bottom Levi's and jackets. After a couple of weeks "in the world" he thought about killing himself "just about every day." Rhodes claimed he came back home as a square peg in a round hole. He didn't fit anywhere. Rhodes kind of shook his head when he told me he had to reenlist in the

Marine Corps for four more years just to be assigned back in snipers at Camp Carroll. On the ship back over to Vietnam, Rhodes actually attempted suicide by slitting his wrists.

I watched Rhodes's face as he told me his story. He didn't look any different than the rest of us. Every marine in Vietnam was expected to kill as many of the enemy as possible if the opportunity was there. Every sniper in his own way wanted to be like Rhodes. To rack up an impressive number of kills and hopefully to return home unchanged.

So what made Rhodes the super-killer we all aspired to be? Maybe he looked for every opportunity—he was hungry for it, and he found it many times. Rhodes told me that night that what made him so damn good was he could smell the enemy long before he ever saw them. We sat on the bunker talking for an hour or better. The evening sky darkened, and light rain changed into a full on downpour. Rhodes suddenly jumped up, standing on the bunker roof, shaking booth fists and screaming at the sky, "Odin, you motherfucker, Oooooooooooooooodin."* He then disappeared down into the bunker still cussing Odin, though in a much quieter voice.

I later learned that Rhodes was killed. He was tail-end Charlie on a sniper patrol down in the valley. He apparently smelled the NVA lying on his back in the tall elephant grass about ten feet off the trail and went to investigate. The story from the marine on the patrol was, from the powder burns around the hole in his forehead, his face was about a foot away when the enemy pulled the trigger on his AK-47.

Toward mid-August, snipers were called to go out with one of the battalions on a large operation ("Prairie II") just south of Con Thien (three kilometers south of the North Vietnam border). This is the same area where I stood on the "big tit" with maggots in my skivvies, seemingly years before. My teammate this time was Tom Lazich. To this day, Tom remains my lifelong friend. Everyone seemed to know that this was going to be a bad one. The heat was going to be a big factor, and there was the strong possibility of making contact with up to a full

---

* Odin, the Norse god associated with war, victory, and death

battalion of battle-ready NVA regulars. This was a sweep and block operation, so as snipers, we expected to hit quite a bit of action.

The road to Con Thien was a straight gouge through brush and low jungle, exposing the ever-present red dirt. I was in a long convoy of 4x4s, with tank support stirring up clouds of red dust, when suddenly all the vehicles came to a stop, and for about one second everything went quiet.

Then it started. Almost as my feet hit the ground, there was an explosion. A marine walking ahead of us in the convoy had hit a bouncing Betty when he left the roadway and started down a trail.* *Shit, this is going to be a bad one. I feel this one in my guts.* It is an inexplicable feeling, to go against primal intuitive warnings when there is absolutely nothing you can do about it.

We made contact with the enemy every day thereafter, and we lost marines every day. Around day four in the operation, Tom and I were in a position about four hundred yards away from the company we were attached to, covering a clearing in a small valley leading to an old rice paddy. Tom was carrying the sniper rifle, and I was spotting.

I could not focus my binoculars, and I felt like hell. By the time a grunt company moved through our position, I was shaking and sweating. After a quick examination, the company corpsman said that I had an extremely high temperature and I needed to be medevaced out immediately.

I have a blurry recollection of holding onto Tom's pack and stumbling back down the trail until we met up with a tank. There were several dead marines on the tank. It was transporting the bodies down to a helicopter-landing zone (LZ) where they could be flown out. There is a blurred memory of jungle and light as I lie on my back on the tank. Once the tank ground to a stop and I was helped down, I could see a line of body bags on the other side of the LZ. I remember hearing the distinctive popping of the rotor blades long before it landed. Lazich helped squeeze me into the already loaded helicopter. I remember seeing bodies and blood and smelling death in the stifling heat as I laid down on the floor of the medevac

---

* Bouncing Bettys are activated by a tripwire and shoot a charge up that explodes about knee to waist high, taking out legs and balls

helicopter. I closed my eyes to avoid the unfortunate cargo as the helo strained to lift off.

Everything in Vietnam was extreme, day after day under the relentless sun. From feeling like you are being steamed alive under your flak jacket by your own sweat, to being chilled to the bone standing watch on endless nights soaked in monsoon rain. There were periods of mind-numbing boredom that switched instantly to having so much adrenaline pumping through your system that your heart felt as if it would explode.

So it was for me in mid-summer 1967, just a few miles south of the DMZ. In a matter of several hours, I went from an environment that was truly hell on earth, to a place where, for a short while until my fever broke, I thought I'd crossed through the gates of heaven. This place was cool and clean and quiet—at least there were no explosions or gunfire, just voices out in the foggy distance.

19

Iwas medevaced to the hospital ship USS *Sanctuary*, cruising along the Vietnam coast, picking up casualties like me who were flown in by medevac helicopters.*

USS Sanctuary AH-17**

Dear folks,

I guess you are wondering why I haven't written lately. I was medevaced from that operation I told you about. I've got malaria. Nothing to worry about though, I am getting good care. I am a little weak yet. The doctor said I should be over it in about a month. Mom, look at it this way, I won't be going on any operations for a while. I've got a rack with sheets, and chow in the rack. So don't worry, I'll be okay. Send my mail to snipers; they in turn will forward it to me. Tell the relatives the circumstances because I won't be able to write them for a while. I'll send you a long letter as soon as I get stronger. This malaria sure takes a lot out of a guy. I love you all very much and I will try to get a letter to Grandma Lock.

Love,

John

USS Sanctuary AH-17***

Dearest family,

I am feeling much better now. My temperature is normal and I am eating again. I have no bad effects except I lost a little weight. The ship is sailing for the Philippine Islands on Sunday for 10 days or so. (The air-conditioning units needed repaired) We are in Danang Harbor, the sun is shining brightly. The water is crystal clear. Just the tranquility of the scene is enough to make a person feel better. I'm not sure what I put in my last letter. I had quite a temperature then, and I wasn't thinking too clearly. I was just worried since I hadn't written

---

* Years later when the Veterans Administration was looking into my file and combat history, they reported that they could find no history of me having malaria, or being on the USS *Sanctuary*.
** Written on the ship's letterhead. No date given.
*** Written on the ship's letterhead. No date given.

in so long. The Sanctuary is basically the same as the Repose, except it has been modernized just a little more. One thing is that it has air-conditioning. When I first got here, I about froze my butt off. Another luxury the Repose didn't have is a TV. For those who can't leave the ward, they can show the movie to them at night. One of the problems I had when I was first up and around was the chow. I shrunk my stomach for several reasons. 1-less chow to pack around, 2-to keep the weight to a minimum, so I was confronted with all this food piled on my tray, chicken, potatoes, gravy, corn, assorted salad and cold milk. I tried so hard to eat it all-my eyes were just bigger than my stomach. Slowly but surely I am able to eat more and more. Also I am getting caught up on my reading. I haven't read a newspaper for three weeks. I can't believe how much of the news the papers leave out. Since it is over for me anyway, I'll tell you why my letters are so scarce and vague the past few weeks. I was part of a full scale operation on the DMZ. The purpose was to push the enemy over the line and hold them there until the elections were held September 3rd. That's why I sent that post-card. It was off of an ammo box and it was all I had to write on. I'm not sure if it will ever reach you, but save it; another Marine Corps first-Ha.

Love,
John

I have the card now in front of me, and it measures roughly 3 x 5 inches. Sniper ammunition comes in a cardboard box with twenty rounds in it. In large letters in the background is the word "Match," an eagle with spread wings and a shield on its chest with blue top and red and white stripes. Its talons clutch arrows on the left, and an olive branch on the right. Printing says it is from the Frankford Arsenal.

On this packing label I wrote:

"Dear folks, on operation-so stationary is nonexistent-this is a note to let you know everything is OK. This whole month has been nothing but operations-I hope Sep, is slower. I should be back that first week in Sep.-so I'll write you a long one then-you ought to frame this-because if this gets to you it's going to be a wonder.
Love John PS mom, stop worrying.

USS Sanctuary AH-17*

---

* Written on the ship's letterhead. No date given.

... Somehow I have the feeling that the war won't last too much longer, with the continual bombing by the B-52s, artillery and high losses when they engage us—they have to be running low on troops. We have found bodies that couldn't have been more than 13 years old. Also we have found Caucasians among the dead that could only mean that they have Russian supervisors or soldiers of fortune. I have already told you of the Chinese or Mongolians they have found. Like I said there is a lot more that goes on than meets the public's eye ...

About the same time I was being medevaced to *Sanctuary*, 3rd Marine Regimental Scout/Snipers were receiving their first Starlight scopes. As things turned out, I never got to take the Starlight scope out into the field. I looked through it a few times when we were at Camp Carroll, and some of the guys were going out on an ambush with it. This was the Holy Grail of sniper technology for the time; having the ability to go out at night with a two-man team, on a moonless night, and be able to spot and take out the enemy. Every sniper team who took the Starlight scope into the field took a white phosphorus hand grenade with them.

Taking the Starlight scope into the field was a major responsibility. It came with a solemn understanding that if there was imminent threat of being captured or killed, the sniper team was to destroy the scope first, with the grenade. It was also understood there was no need to come back to Camp Carroll if, for some reason, you didn't have the Starlight in your possession.

USS Sanctuary AH-17*

My Dearest Family,

We should be arriving in the Philippines in the next few hours. We started out in rough seas, and to tell you the truth I felt a tad ill for the first few hours. After I got my sea legs, I really enjoyed the trip, especially the sunsets. You couldn't imagine all the colors. Yesterday we had a cookout on the helicopter landing pad. Steaks and the whole bit. Promise not to tell anyone? I went through the line 3 times. I remember thinking this has to be like heaven. I was out there in the hot jungle and sick, and now as I'm feeling better the ship is sailing for the Philippines. That I have my appetite back, and I'm able to see

---

* Written on the ship's letterhead. No date given.

the sun sets, and cook steaks, and have clean sheets, is far beyond my imagination. I just couldn't imagine anything finer. My doctor told me I was a first-class patient, so I'll get to pull liberty without restrictions. Although the only money I'll have is eight dollars, I am sure to have fun. We are going to spend about 14 days here and they are going to pay us a small amount during that time. Dad, I guess I told you that the Starlight scopes came into snipers the day I was medevaced. My very best friend, Walter Smith, "Smitty" came down to see me just before I went on the operation. He works in S3 section. He used to be in F. Company 2nd Battalion 3rd Marines along with me. He worries about me as bad as you do, Mom. Before an operation he is always checking my gear, putting in extra socks and goodies he has saved. Being in S3, he can follow all the reports, so he knows where I am all the time. I got Smitty out of sort of a hot situation one time when he was wounded, and he just won't forget it. He is a great guy and we have a lot of plans as far as school goes and travel. He was on one of the tapes I sent home, remember? I don't know how I got carried away like this–oh well, I'll let you know how much fun in the sun goes.

Love,

John

In a time when "weird shit" happened on a daily basis, the ten days I spent in Subic Bay, Philippine Islands, had to rate very high on the weird shit list. Once *Sanctuary* tied up in Subic Bay, most ambulatory patients were given a "Cinderella liberty." We could get off the ship at 10 a.m. and had to be back by 5 p.m. Not having any uniforms, we were issued a set of khakis. So we all hit town as privates; even most old salts didn't bother sewing on their chevrons. I said in my letter I didn't have much money, but I remember that they issued us half of our monthly base pay; for me it was about forty dollars. A chief petty officer told us that we could not go out on liberty if we did not have any money. He warned us if we went out, got drunk, got rolled, and lost all of our money, which was very common in Olongapo City, "your ass will be confined to the ship for the rest of the time in port."

The first morning out, I was almost giddy with excitement. This was a bustling city full of life, with a reputation of being one of the most decadent in the Philippine Islands. After months of extreme existence in the bush, this was an extreme of a whole other world. The streets were filled with pedicabs, bicycles, and many very colorful, highly stylized taxis. Every sidewalk was filled with people, vendors, and market stalls. It didn't take very long for the many exotic smells and sounds and the crush of people to start to close in on me.

I stopped momentarily on the corner of a busy intersection; I wanted to get off the street and have a cold beer. A middle-aged Filipino woman with a big-eyed little girl holding tightly to her leg pulled on my sleeve and offered her eight- to ten-year-old daughter to give me a "number one blow job—only five dollar." I looked into their faces, and I felt a sick panic inside. I had to get out of that situation fast. Man, I wasn't ready for this at all. I ducked into the bar right behind me, which was up a flight of stairs, on the second story of a building located on the corner of a busy intersection.

It was still before noon and I didn't see anyone in the place except the bartender and a couple of girls over at the far end of the bar. The chairs were all turned up on the tables, and I took a chair down from the table next to the window overlooking the intersection. This was a great vantage point to see what was going on without getting crushed. I ordered a beer.

One of the girls brought a beer over and said, "Hey, Marine, you buy me drinky?" In hindsight the events that followed may have been the direct result of my "wet behind the ears, 'cherry boy' mentality." I said, "No, I can't afford it." I told her I was a patient on a hospital ship. I explained the situation about having to make less than fifty dollars last almost two weeks, or I wouldn't be able to get off the ship. I talked to her like she was the girl next door. I took my money out of my wallet and showed it to her. I told her I hadn't talked with a lady in a long time, and if she got a glass, I would share my beer with her.

We talked for a least an hour and shared several beers. She wasn't drop-dead gorgeous. She reminded me more of a Filipino farm girl with exotic dark brown eyes. Her two teeth next to the top front teeth were capped in gold with hearts etched out in the middle, revealing her white teeth. She had a great laugh.

I was about ready to order another beer when she said in a soft voice, "Why don't we go up to room?" I reminded her of my financial situation, and she said, "No, me take care." She took me by the hand and led me through a door at the end of the bar, up some stairs, and into a surprisingly clean and well-appointed small room. The following blissful hours seemingly evaporated, and I found myself sprinting back to *Sanctuary* with a big smile on my face and a feeling of utter disbelief. She made me promise that I would come back the moment I got off the ship the next day.

I couldn't help but share the story of my good fortune with my ward mates back on the ship. I long ago forgot the name of one guy in this group who bunked just down from me. He was a French Canadian who joined the Marine Corps to get his United States citizenship. He was a bear of a man. He had black hair all over his body, and he was big and kind of round like a bear. He had multiple small shrapnel wounds and a couple of big wounds with major stitches. He couldn't pull liberty until his stitches came out. In sharing the events of my good fortune, I left out the most intimate details. Just the idea that I had spent the afternoon with a willing and eager female was almost too much for him.

Bear Man was suffering from a near terminal case of French Canadian blue balls. He also had at least three or four days to go before his stitches came out and they let him off the ship. Every day I would go back to the bar, to my same table by the window, and share several beers, some great conversation, and a lot of laughs with the same Filipino girl. When she was ready, without saying anything, she would stand up and take my hand, and lead me to a place that could only be called Shangri-La.

The next afternoon, while we were feeding each other pineapple slices in the room, I told her about my French Canadian friend and his need to find a nice Filipino girl once his stitches were out. She said she knew the perfect girl. So we planned kind of a "getting off the ship party" for him.

That night I told my hairy Canadian shipmate of our plans. I still have the memory of the look on his face. His whole face stiffened up and his nostrils flared. Although he didn't think my reaction to this was funny, he really cracked me up.

It took a couple of more days before his stitches came out for him to get off the ship. By that time our plans were etched in stone. My Canadian friend was able to collect several hundred dollars back pay off the books. We reserved the best two rooms above the bar; we had ordered a bottle of whiskey and champagne and a catered lunch for four.

The minute the liberty bell sounded that morning, I practically had to double-time to keep up with him as we burned a trail into Olongapo. We were within a half a block of the bar when the most beautiful Asian flower I had ever seen stepped from a doorway and said, "Hi, Marines." We both stopped dead in our tracks. By the time my heart skipped a beat, the Bear was already standing next to her. I don't think he heard anything I said to him after that, except that I'd be in the bar and I pointed up the stairs.

When I met my girl in the bar and told her what happened, she and her friend were very disappointed. What could I say? I was ambushed. Best laid plans and all that. A short time later, the Canadian showed up with this gorgeous Asian beauty who could easily have been a movie star. We had some beers and drinks at my "usual" table and got acquainted.

My girl was unusually quiet and said hardly a thing. I just passed it off as being upset about her girlfriend she'd brought for the French Canadian being stood up. Before long we made our way up to our "penthouse rooms" where we had several more drinks, but passed on the food for the time being. Quite soon the doors between our rooms were shut.

Once I had snuggled down with my girl, she turned to me and said, "Is your friend a queer?"

"Is he what?"

"A queer, a fag, you know? Your friend has a Benny boy," she responded.

Before I was able to ask her what the hell a "Benny boy" was, there was a big crash from the next room. I jumped from the bed and flung open the adjoining door just as this 220-pound plus Canadian bear caught this ninety-pound Benny boy by the meat on his chest, and tried slamming him through the wall.

In the next instant both rooms were filled with Filipinos. Some hustled the howling Benny boy out the door, while others tried to calm down a truly, insanely enraged bear, French Canadian, United States Marine.

When he turned around and looked at me, I had never seen a more insane look. His veins were standing out on his forehead, and his voice had kind of a choked quality when he said to me, "Nutting, if you ever say a fucking word to anyone back at the ship, or ever, for that matter, I swear to God I will slit your throat and throw your ass overboard." There was never a doubt in my mind that he meant every word of it.

Although we had five or six more days of liberty, we never went out together again. In fact the next day he moved to an empty bunk at the other end of the squad bay. For the rest of the time on *Sanctuary*, we only nodded to each other when we made eye contact.

I spent every moment I could with the generous, loving, and kind-hearted Filipino bar girl, and now after all these years, I can't even remember her name. I was still a few weeks away from my twenty-first birthday, and I think I started to love her, because it hurt when I had to go.

Every night was a sleepless night on the voyage back to Vietnam. I walked long hours through the many corridors of the ship. I joined the same faces with dark-circled eyes, smoking cigarettes in the head,* night after night at 0300 hours. All the night zombies were combat veterans, getting ready to go back into the shit. I knew how lucky I had been so far. How many near misses and close calls had I had? How many more times would a bullet crack just past my head? How many more body bags would I put on a medevac before it was my turn? I knew in an instant a marine could be doomed to living a life without any legs and having a catheter for what used to be a penis. I passed the same wards filled with the same horrifically wounded young men as I saw on *Repose*. I wanted to survive *intact* even more.

There was so much life I hadn't experienced. It had been so good to be in that little room with the tender-hearted Filipino bar girl. It had been the best. It was so good to feel the freedom of not being in a combat zone and having that feeling that you could be in someone's crosshairs. To have the freedom to laugh out loud, to eat good food, drink cold beer, to make love to an eager woman, what more could anyone want in life, ever?

---

* Latrine

20

Big changes were made with the snipers by the time I made it back to Camp Carroll from USS *Sanctuary* in mid-August 1967. Gunnery Sergeant Costello was gone; no one collected the MPC's in the jar. "Gunny" was replaced by a young captain.

I know some changes happened within me during the time I was recovering from malaria. I still had a cold darkness that welled up in dreams at night and in unexpected times of solitude. I prayed that if I only got one confirmed kill while I was in Vietnam, that it would be the NVA who was setting booby traps around the village of Than Dinh Son. I still wanted payback; I still felt like I needed that revenge.

I tried hard. However, every time I carried the Remington 700, if we even saw the enemy, they were just disappearing over the hill or were just out of range or it was too dangerous to take a shot.

The other change within me was a growing sense of apathy. We were not going to make any great changes for the Vietnamese people—at least not during my tour. We were still losing marines on the same ground we had fought on when I was a grunt nine months before. I had seen too much already. I did not want to go home in a box or worse yet, without my legs and my balls.

I teamed back up with my old friend Bjorn Dahlin when I got back to Camp Carroll. I wanted to get back down into the Delta Five area as soon as possible where the sapper got my squad, and Bjorn was gung ho about everything. He was more than ready to go after that son of a bitch too, but he wasn't too sure about me. After all, he reasoned, I was just recouping from a bout of malaria, and after almost a month of hot chow and clean sheets, I had probably gotten real soft.

Bjorn truly was the "Sergeant Rock" of our unit, the man with the most overall field time by far. This is no kidding: he had me double-timing with him around the paths and roads inside Camp Carroll, if we were not out in the field. He showed me karate moves and had me toughen up my hands on sandbags. He showed me unique hand-to-hand combat techniques; one was a swift move that had me instantly in a fetal position, gasping for air in the red dust.

Once monsoon season started—at least in the beginning of the season— I didn't go out into the field as often. Many times I had two or three days of downtime. I was able to catch up on letter writing and cutting hair, and on a more and more frequent basis, I went down into the bunker by myself.

Most of us got our "stash" from an ex-Mormon missionary and mess-hall cook, who traded C rations for "reefers" with the Vietnamese when he went on a supply run to Danang.

Getting to go down into the bunker after an operation or patrol was like the carrot on a stick. It was a special hour or so in a dark space in the ground, but most importantly it meant you had made it back. A bunker was a place where you could find refuge from mortar rounds or sometimes a place for quiet solitude. I remember several times when I took one of those little joints and disappeared into the cool quiet of a bunker, enjoying a peaceful time of being invisible, anonymous, and embracing the pitch dark blackness as I smoked the joint down to where I could feel the heat on my fingers and lips.

October 1, 1967

Dear Mom and Dad and Kiddies,

Well like you said mom, Sunday is a poor day to write letters. It looks as if the summer rainy season has now turned into the winter monsoon season. Gads the mud is all over the place. It looks just like last year. People slipping, sliding and falling. It is impossible to stay clean for long. They are still messing around with my pay records, so I guess I'll go to Dong Ha tomorrow and see the dispensing officer about my pay. I should have in the neighborhood of $278. Do you realize that it was a year ago that I was home on leave? Sure doesn't seem like a full year since we were together... Well, I'm rolling in the money again and not from gambling. I am cutting hair in my spare time. Today I made $9.50. That's not bad considering I'm not allowed by a divisional order to charge anything. So, not to be outdone, in my plan I just put out a tip box, so there is no way I can get hung. And what's more, there is a lifer who cuts hair, one style only, Marine Corps skinhead. So to take his business away, I cut all styles. Mail call and I just got one letter. It was from a guy that I was on the Sanctuary with. He was sent home the day I went back onto the Hill. He had TB of the kidneys. A great guy-too bad about his filters though. Ya know something, each day I realize what a great job you did in bringing me up. I've always hated being pushed into something and you very rarely pushed me. Religion is something you can't push on anyone; it's just too deep a subject. Being over here I have become very close to God. Could you imagine what a jam I would be in if I didn't know how to pray when things get bad and I get the shit scared out of me; there is nothing more ensuring than to say a prayer. ... Damn, they had rat stew (mystery meat) again with asparagus and rice-always rice, never a day without rice. I've lost my gift for gab back at the mess hall must've been the rice. I feel like writing a poem* tonight.

Love to All,
John

---

* I wrote poems in high school and all the time in the Marines. I had signed up for a three-year tour—I did have a two-year option—so that after my obligatory Vietnam tour (two years) I might be assigned to *Stars and Stripes* in the extra year as a reporter/writer. This was promised by the recruiter. And, of course, it didn't happen.

21

About the time the monsoon hit, hardback tents were being put up around Camp Carroll. These more permanent buildings were replacing some of the main officers' quarters; civilization was coming to Camp Carroll. One of the old officers' tents had been converted into a makeshift enlisted men's club, and they were actually shipping beer up to us from Danang on most supply runs. In the last letter, I wrote about the mud and the muck, which was ever present during the rainy season. But certainly it was not like when I first arrived almost a year before, when Camp Carroll was a raw red gouge on a plateau. Even then, Camp Carroll with its rough, bulldozed emplacements, in the heavy, sticky red mud and guys drying their clothes around the burning shitters seemed like a much more civilized place, compared with the rat-infested bunkers at Con Thien.

It was during this time of transition around Camp Carroll—when most of the old, heavily worn tents were being taken down, and new tents were being erected—that my tour in Vietnam took another unexpected turn.

I had just returned to Camp Carroll, from a few days out in the field. We were on a particularly taxing patrol, constantly on the move. I was exhausted. I had barely removed my pack when word came down that "every swinging dick" had just been volunteered to move the colonel's tent. It was late in the afternoon, and it had been raining for days, when suddenly there was a break in the weather and the sun came out. The colonel wanted the whole "shitterree" moved to higher ground before it started raining again.

The colonel's tent had been erected over a floor of shipping pallets. As luck would have it, I stuck my hand into a rats nest as I attempted to move one of the pallets, and I felt a sharp pain—a bite. A large rat streaked across an open muddy area, disappearing into a bunker as I checked out my finger. I hoped there might be a possibility that I just scratched it on a nail, but our corpsman said the wound looked too much like a bite to take any chances, and since we didn't kill the rat, I needed to go see the head "Doc" on the plateau.

I liked the Doc right off. He looked to be only a few years older than me and had a very wired-up personality. This rabies business was very exciting to him. I was immediately put on light duty, and the next day, the Doc called me in for a conference. He said a fresh injection, packed in dry ice, would be flown up by helicopter every morning with mail call. Doc explained to me that he would give me an injection in the fat around my belly button every morning and that it was going to hurt like hell. He also informed me that he had to do this for twenty-one consecutive days and for that period of time, I would be on light duty because there was a possibility the injection could give me encephalitis.

He was right; the injections felt like someone had left a burning cigarette on my stomach for about a minute. The first few days of light duty gave me a chance to get caught up on writing letters and squaring away my gear. Two or three days into the injections, Tom Lazich reported in from the field with a dog bite. Actually, it was a puppy he was playing with. The Doc said Tom needed the rabies shots also, so we were assigned to keep an eye on each other for signs of encephalitis.

Every morning on my way to sick bay I usually stopped off at the mess hall to get a cup of black coffee and to prepare myself for a big dose of pain. Tom got his injection in the late afternoon. The first week was easy street, playing poker, eating, sleeping, reading, or going down into the bunker. Surprisingly enough, all this free time became very boring and increasingly depressing in a way. I remember feeling an odd kind of envy when some of the guys would be saddling up to go out on a patrol.

22

Dear Folks,

It looks as if my skating days are over. By showing everyone my superhuman feats in doing push-ups, somebody must've realized that I wasn't in as much pain as I let on, so I am on mess duty, washing greasy, smelly, grimy old pots. Oh, man. Fourteen hours a day for two weeks-scrubbing pots.

Swede had this knife that he was presented with when he graduated from the Swedish commandos. It is a combat knife worn on his leg. It's ugly as hell. It's been in three conflicts: the Congo, Cyprus and Vietnam. It has also killed two men in the Congo. He has had it almost nine years, and I suppose it is his most treasured possession. Last night Swede gave me his knife as a token of our friendship. I didn't know what to do. I didn't really want to take it, but what could I do? I didn't want to hurt his feelings. Now, I have the problem of returning a token to him. *Damn, I just realize what I've written and it sounds like some cornball writing to Dear Abby. Vikki tomorrow is your birthday. I just hope your gifts get there in time. Maybe you'll write me a small thank-you note since you won't write me any other time. To my little brother I say, "Hey numb nuts, how's the arm?" Man, I can see you just hamming it up to get sympathy from all those squirrelly little girlies ...

Love,

John

---

* Years later, in 1998 or 1999 Swede called me up to ask me if I would be interested in meeting him at the local casino where the traveling Vietnam Wall would be on display for several days. Both Bjorn and I had been unsuccessful in visiting the Wall when it came to our respective towns; it was just too emotionally difficult. He thought maybe if we went together, we could be successful.

The evening before Swede and I were to rendezvous, for some reason I remembered Swede's combat knife down in the bottom of my sea bag, where it had been for thirty-five years or so, and in my heart I knew this was the time to return it. After meeting the next day we decided to have a cup of coffee in the casino before we ventured over to the Wall. During a pause in our "getting caught up conversation," and without saying anything, I pulled his knife out of my backpack and slid it across the table to him.

I saw flickers of many emotions cross my brother's face, before he finally smiled and nodded with a peaceful acceptance. We found strength in being in each other's company, and we were able to locate the names of our many fallen friends and brothers, and take a few rubbings.

The pot-scrubbing shack was a little building just down the hill from the mess hall, supply tents, and dishwashing area. From the pot shack was a breathtaking view sweeping down into the valley, with Hue on the far southern horizon. The pot shack became our hangout, a safe haven—our little space. Nobody messed with you when you worked the pot shack. As long as the greasy pots and pans came back relatively clean, nobody came down there.

Many nights, several of us—along with the ex-Mormon cook—would go down in the bunker by the pot shack, smoke some of his reefer, and eat some purloined goodies from the mess hall. On top of the bunker with our panoramic view, we could see tracers from the firefights going on, explosions, and distant flashes reflecting off the clouds.

* * * *

Humor comes during war in strange forms. Vietnam was no different. The funniest event I witnessed while I was in Vietnam happened while I was working in the pot shack.

A couple of months previously, the Army Corps of Engineers had dug a hole next to the mess hall about the size of the basement for a small house. This was filled with rock and gravel. The pit was used for a drain field for all the gray water coming from the mess hall. This hole had also become a destination resort for a few thousand rats. In just a short time the little bits of food washed from food servers that drained down between the rocks turned the pit into a major rat gourmet center and breeding ground.

The mess hall was run by a ruddy faced, white-haired lifer staff sergeant who was partial to whiskey. One afternoon, those of us fortunate enough to be working in the pot shack observed the mess sergeant and two mess-duty PFCs, each with a five-gallon Jerry can, headed toward the motor pool.*

When the detail came back from the motor pool, the old mess sergeant directed the PFCs to dump the gas all over the rocks, down the sides, and

---

* Gasoline was stored near the motor pool in a very large, flat rubber bladder—maybe eighteen inches to two feet in height, and very wide so that if a mortar round hit it there was a good chance it would absorb the shock and bounce off.

into the corners of the drain field; he wanted full coverage. Then he yelled at his helpers to stand back because he was going to, "git every one of those miserable sons-a-bitches." The sergeant lit a torch made out of a rolled-up newspaper and threw it on the drain field.

Instantly, there was a huge explosion and a rapidly rising fireball. Rocks and flaming rats filled the air. Then several things happened simultaneously. There, still standing close to the drain field, was the quite-scorched mess sergeant with a look of total disbelief on his face. The still-living rats were running everywhere—some on fire or smoking. Seconds later the "incoming siren" started screeching, sending everyone scrambling for the bunkers.

Maybe it was just one of those things that you had to be there to witness, but to watch it all unfold within yards in front of us was the funniest thing that any of us had seen in a very long time. Needless to say the colonel was not pleased, and the shit hit the fan on several levels.

A couple of days later, the Army Corps of Engineers came in and created a new drain field, covering the old blasted-out hole. About two weeks after that, the mess sergeant, now a buck sergeant, came back from the hospital in Danang, recovering from the burns on his face and hands, with patches of new pink skin, and minus the rocker on his Chevron.

23

Dearest Family,

. . . As of today I'm the shortest* man in the platoon. I'm the last of the old timers to leave. Keyes, Wright, and Pittman all left early this morning. They had a ceremony for me last night. I was presented with the short-timers cover**; only I am allowed to wear it. It has all the guys' signatures that rotated before me on it. I was also presented with this short-timer's walking stick, and a short-timer's soda that has never been opened and has only about a half an ounce in it. When I leave I will add my name to these treasures and passed it on to the next short-timer. I just realize something-it is exactly one year ago to the minute that I was getting on that big silver bird and going back to Camp Pendleton for Staging. So depending on how ya look at it, it doesn't seem like a year at all. Mom, if a whole year goes by that fast/just think how fast these next few weeks will go by. I hope you are counting the days, because I am not. When I was counting them, it made the days go so much slower. Everyone on the Hill is screaming their heads off about the mail. It is just getting pretty bad when only a few letters come up to the plateau each day. Oh, well, I know you will be getting my letters and that's all that matters now. My stomach is beginning to feel like an impact area for the B-52s, and I'm only halfway through, but at least I'm staying on the plateau, and as long as I'm staying behind the lines, I'm happy. I'm writing this at my desk—that's the pot shack. It seems the only time I have to write is during work hours, so I hope I don't get caught. I'm going to a party tonight. One of the doctors is going home, so free beer at the club tonight. This Doc is just like one of the regular peons. One morning I went to get my shot and he was gassed, his breath smelled like a hundred proof, and on top of it he had to take the Colonel's tonsils out that night. Man—I just about cracked up when he told me that! We were both cracking up when he gave me the shot. It's a wonder he didn't cut off the Colonel's tongue.

I think all the long hours of mindlessly washing greasy pots gave me a lot of time to think about my situation. I didn't want to be one of those guys who

---

*   I had less time remaining than any other of my buddies
**   A hat

were killed in the last couple of weeks of their tour. Enlisted men are allowed only one R&R during their 13 month tour, and I had already gone to Taipei Taiwan in March. If could somehow figure out how to go on another R&R it would take up 10 days or so that I could conceivably go back into the field.

Love,
John

November 4, 1967

Dearest Family,

Here I am again with my evening newsletter. Today I mailed boxes totaling 46 pounds. It has miscellaneous gear from knives to utilities. Also the mail brought me the money I asked for so I'll quit bugging you about it. Another letter was from a very close friend of mine, Charlie Keys.* He was the one I wrote about who rotated last month. It was sort of depressing. He said people back in the world just didn't give a damn about the people over here. He also said "it's sort of funny John, just 18 days ago you and I were setting in the rain hoping to kill someone and now I'm a civilian. I feel like such a social outcast—it's going to be a long, long while before I get adjusted to the civilian life again." I am a little dubious myself about adjusting to civilian life again. That's one thing I have thought about a lot. I hope I can adjust while I am home on leave. It's going to take a lot of hard work on my part, and a lot of understanding on yours. I just hope I don't flub up around the Locks or some of the more tender relatives. If you haven't read the papers for a while I'll tell you another scosh of news: we have been awarded another ribbon, the presidential unit citation for heroism and gallantry for operation Prairie II—that's the one I was wounded in. Well, with this nightly letter I can just barely eke out the pages, but you know I am thinking of you always. It's good night for now, keep counting Ma, it won't be long now.

Love,
John

---

* Charlie Keys was, without a doubt, one of the most intelligent people the snipers ever had. I learned both his parents were scientists, and Charlie had a photographic memory. He told me in confidence one time when we were down in the bunker that he was a member of Mensa. Charlie was my very close friend. I've tried to get a hold of him. But Charlie has no phone and never returns any mail. He is a recluse who lives by himself in a cabin way back in the woods in Northern California.

Sometimes we would have a poker game with the army artillery guys. The army had the huge 175 artillery pieces that would fire missions all the damn time. We were all paid with military payment certificates (MPC). It kind of looked like glorified Monopoly money, and money didn't really mean a doodle anyway because we didn't have any place to spend it. Sometimes the pots got pretty high. One of the army guys introduced a new game—it was new to me, anyway. And it was called acey-deucy. The short of it is, I won almost $300.

It cost me $65 to have a cutthroat sergeant put my name at the top of the R&R list. He started out wanting a hundred bucks.

[mid-November 1967]

Dearest Family,

Today is a black day for me. I just found out that my R&R flight date has been changed from November 28th to December 3rd. I am due to rotate from this hole on December 10th. I'll have to go down to the company office tomorrow and see if I can get it changed or I could just forget it completely--hell, I'd save money. I just don't know. Not much news today. Except from where I stand to watch pots, I have a complete view of the whole valley. The small village of Dong Ha got hit with about 200 artillery rounds. I watched the whole thing while washing pots. One highlight was the gooks hit the ammo dump. Damn! It looked like Dong Ha was one big column of black smoke. They hit the same dump when I was on the USS Sanctuary. All sorts of debris was scattered all over the place. It's all in a day's work, I guess. . . .

Love,

John

We were hit very hard at the very end of my time in the pot shack. However, not as hard as Dong Ha. Danang and Cam Lo both took heavy hits during the end of November.

24

We were getting hit hard the day I was due to leave for R&R in Bangkok, Thailand. The NVA were trying to knock out some of the Army's 175 mm artillery. Consequently, a large number of RPG and mortar rounds landed in the sniper area on the plateau adjacent to where these gun-carrying tanks were parked.

We didn't take any casualties, but it was enough to keep everyone hunkered down in their bunkers for most of the day and into the night. Only the medevac helicopters came in to the plateau that day.

There was no more pot shack; it had taken a direct hit. It had been a close call to start the day for me and the marines located in a bunker almost directly in front of where the pot shack had once been. I knew then I probably wasn't going to get off the plateau, and have a transition day in Danang.

Once in Danang, usually the first thing a marine going on R&R would do was retrieve his sea bag from division headquarters. Next he would go to a laundry mama-san to get the fungus washed out of his khakis and have his dress shoes spit shined by one of her kids. Next door, he would get a shave and a haircut. Only then would he check in his rifle at the armory on the way to the enlisted men's club. It was well-known that as soon as a marine finished checking in, he was able get a head start on his R&R down in the enlisted men's club by drinking 25-cent cold beers or mixed drinks with ice.

Early the next morning the word came down the line that "if Nutting wants to go on R&R, have him grab his shit, and get down to the LZ [landing zone], ASAP." I grabbed what little gear I had, and double-timed to the LZ, just barely jumping on board the waiting helicopter. My elation at actually catching the helicopter quickly subsided when I saw the only cargo besides me was two body bags among several large mailbags and a stone-faced door gunner who never looked my way once we took to the air.

I guess, for lack of a better word, the whole thing made me feel creeped out. I had survived to see another sunrise, and I was on my way to get righteously drunk, hopefully stoned, and possibly laid. The boys at my feet were a couple of army guys who got the shit rocketed out of their gun emplacements. I think during that flight to Danang I had some of my first flashbacks, although I would have said then that I was just having some very vivid memories.

Once my helicopter touched down in Danang, I had to double-time the moment my foot hit the blacktop. My plane to Bangkok was already loading on the tarmac and and the guy at the check-in said, "Go—they're holding the plane for you." I grabbed my orders, checked my weapon, and ran to the plane. The airplane was a civilian Pan-American Airlines jet that had just unloaded a planeload of new guys. As I walked down the aisle in my pot-shack grunge jungle utilities, I saw spiffed-out, shiny-faced marines in clean khakis stopping in midsentence to look at me.

It had probably been at least several days since I had shaved and who knows how long since I had showered. Only within the last month or six weeks had they installed a gravity-fed shower at Camp Carroll. It was a shower with water warmed by the sun that was used mostly by the officers—otherwise it was bathing in a river, out of your helmet, or sometimes in a good rainstorm.

An older stewardess—not all that attractive to me but still very seductive—guided me to an empty seat at the very end of the aircraft, next to a marine sitting by himself. As the plane became airborne and the stewardesses passed out rounds of drinks to the mildly rowdy marines, the marine next to me confided in me about a dilemma he was facing. He told me his name was Joe. He was in recon, about six months into his tour, and just had to get out of the country for a breather. He said he was starting to "freak out—way too much pressure."

Joe told me he had married his high school sweetheart. He knew that if he got drunk he would want to get a girl and get laid. And there was no way that he was going on R&R and not getting drunk. I told him that I had most likely decided that I didn't want a girl at all. I was a very short,

short-timer. I had heard all the stories about the infamous "black syphilis, incurable drippy dick, and terminal anal warts," and I did not want anything to delay my going home for Christmas. I also told him that my friend Walt Smith told me every single detail of his R&R in Bangkok at least three times, including the fact that Bangkok was "that gem-buying center of the world." My main mission, besides getting out of the country, was to find some very cool Christmas presents for my family.

The stewardess that was in the tail section of our plane was kind of platinum blonde and older—like maybe thirty-three or thirty-four. I had never looked at an older woman and seen what I was seeing; she had something extra, something I hadn't observed in a woman older than myself before. She had this magnetic smile when she made eye contact, and the way she moved around in the plane with such style and class kept all the jarheads in the tail section acting like a bunch of well-behaved schoolboys. About midway into the flight she was standing next to me and said, "Marine, you smell bad. Where did you come from?" I told her I was stationed at Camp Carroll, and by the look on her face I felt she knew where Camp Carroll was. She gave me her beautiful smile, with dark rose-colored lips and perfect white teeth, and then informed me that she was going to give me a shave.

I have an exceptionally clear memory of being in that airplane with my eyes closed, smelling her perfume, occasionally hearing her breath in my ear, and a couple of times feeling her soft breast lightly touch my shoulder. This had to be one of those "only in Vietnam" kind of days. I started out my morning with someone hoping to kill me with a rocket, flying out in a helicopter with a couple of body bags, and now I'm getting shaved by a buxom, blond American, full-bodied, Marilyn Monroe–type stewardess, and it wasn't even noon yet.

25

I thought I was going to suffocate in the packed holding room at the Bangkok airport before a pimply-faced, Gomer-looking, air force desk jockey finished his indoctrination lecture. We again heard the warning of all the different kinds of incurable venereal diseases and not to stray from the US-inspected hooker bars. He also warned us that everything in Bangkok—bars, hotels, jewelry stores, restaurants, hookers, everything—was a member of one syndicate or another. He said the first thing you do is *not* hire a cab driver for the full week, otherwise you'll wind up going only to the places that are part of his syndicate and that we would definitely not get the best deals. With the lecture finished, we were loaded onto various shuttle buses and taken us to our hotels located around Bangkok. Smitty had made me promise that I would go to the Amanchai Hotel—the same place he stayed when he was on R&R. Joe, the recon marine who set next to me in the plane, decided that's where he would like to go also, so eventually we got rooms next to each other.

In hindsight my room wasn't all that exceptional by today's standards, but at the time, I felt like I was walking through the gates of paradise. The main room was rather small, but it did have a large bed with a television set, a sliding glass door that opened on to a small balcony looking out onto a courtyard with many tropical plants and a small swimming pool. The bathroom could have been something out of one of my better dreams. For its compact size, it had an oversized sunken tile bathtub. On the wall was a high-tech speaker for its time, with four channels: Asian, classical, country and western, and rock 'n' roll. This had to be a dream; I felt nothing could feel this good as I slid into the steamy hot, jasmine-scented bubble bath, while over the "too good to be true" speaker, the Beatles sang "Lucy in the Sky with Diamonds."

I had just sunk down into submarine mode, when a loud knock at my door brought me back to reality. It was Joe and with him was a Thai cabdriver who called himself Peter. He wanted to be of "service to us as our first-class cabdriver twenty-four hours a day" for the week that we were there. Peter said he would take us "anywhere, anytime, anyplace," and he would guarantee us the best possible prices anywhere in Bangkok, "all for a very modest price."

I was the reluctant one; the indoctrination lecture made sense to me—why get tied up with one guy for the whole week? There I was in the tub, and Joe was sitting on the commode, drinking some kind of mixed drink, and trying to sing along to the music. In front of me was an extra-hyper Thai cabdriver who was pacing back and forth in full on negotiation mode. I kept thinking to myself, *Man, what happened to the peace and quiet?*

Finally I said, "Peter, can you get me dinky dau* weed? You know, Park Lanes?" Peter said, "Sure, no sweat" and disappeared out the door. The only time I left the comfort of this amazingly wonderful tub of hot water was to take a leak and open another ice-cold beer. Peter returned in no more than twenty minutes with more reefers in a plastic bag than I could smoke in six months. Peter produced a small crooked pipe with a little lid on it. This little pipe was a present for me, "with no strings." Peter put some of the green vegetation in the pipe and handed it to me, since Joe was only interested in getting "D-R-U-N-K and then D-R-U-N-K-E-R." I said, "What the hell?" and took a couple of deep puffs. About thirty seconds later I told Peter he was hired for the full week, which made Joe howl, "Yee-haw!" like some kind of a drunken cowboy.

That evening Peter took us to a nice restaurant for very memorable meal. "The best Thai food in Bangkok." After C rations and Camp Carroll mess hall chow, the fresh seafood and vegetables were truly exquisite. And then we were on to some exotic nightlife.

Joe picked up a girl almost immediately—a moon-faced beauty with a very compact and shapely body. After a while, I noticed a young lady who appeared to be having a great time with all her girlfriends at the end of the bar. So I asked our barmaid to invite her over to join us.

---

* Vietnam-era military slang for "to be crazy"

She introduced herself as Mae. She was very attractive with dark shiny hair, mischievous eyes, and a great smile. Joe's girl and my girl were old friends, so we had a great time dancing and drinking and dancing some more. Joe had been drinking most of the day and was getting pretty wobbly and thick tongued, so it was time to head back to the hotel. I had an unexpected great evening with this "cheeky" young lady. In order to take my girl back to the hotel, I had to sign a contract with mama-san at the bar. The price to have my girl as a companion for twenty-four hours was twelve dollars. The contract said if for any reason I was unhappy with my girl I could bring her back and get a different girl—one time only. Mae later told me that out of that twelve dollars, she received four dollars and fifty cents. The rest went to the bar, the hotel, the cab driver, etc. We said good-night to Joe and his girl and retired to our room in the Amanchai Hotel. I found out the next day that Joe had fallen in his tub that night and cracked open his head. I never saw him again.

Truthfully, more than anything, I was really looking forward to another hot soak in that excellent tub. I was starting to feel the deep body ache of too many hours with not enough sleep.

I had nursed a couple of beers through the evening, but I had long ago sweated them out on the dance floor. I was really looking forward to dipping into the fat bag of Thai weed and soaking away another layer of red dirt, along with the aches—all of the aches—in peaceful steamy bliss.

Like many long and strange days that had occurred in the past year, this day went from one level to another in the blink of an eye. I had no sooner fired up the little pipe with my trusty Zippo lighter when Mae, the bar girl, emerged from the bathroom. I'm holding my breath, savoring probably the best reefer I've ever smoked, when suddenly I'm listening to what sounds like to me a high-speed Thai Minnie Mouse on helium.

Once Mae slowed down and started speaking English, I understood what had flipped her switch. She kept saying, "You smoke devil's smoke, number ten, devil smoke, number ten, devil smoke, number ten, you no smoke, you no smoke." I felt a nice wave flow over me from the reefer as I exhaled, and I knew all I really wanted to do was get into that wonderful peaceful space reefer put me in.

I assured Mae that I was much more interested in seeking Nirvana in the bathtub than having sex with her at the moment, depraved or otherwise. I let her know that she could sleep all night in the bed, and I would not bother her, or she could call Peter to take her back to wherever she wanted to go. With that I headed for round two in the jasmine-scented bubble bath.

I let the darkness wash over me along with the steaming hot water, with only my nose and lips breaking the surface. Sweating out the remaining ground in deep layers of red Vietnamese dirt, I couldn't stop the vivid pictures behind my eyelids, and before I really wanted to, I had to get out. I remember thinking, as I crawled out of the tub and buried my head in a clean towel, about the two soldiers in the body bags. They were probably in steel boxes on their first leg home in the belly of a cargo plane, and I was on my way to a soft rack with clean sheets.

When I came from the bathroom, I was surprised to see Mae fully awake and sitting cross-legged in the middle of the bed in her skivvies and T-shirt. I think Mae was surprised that I hadn't turned into some horny beast and that I had offered her a place to sleep with no strings attached. She started asking me questions about pot, and I told her what little I knew: that it affected people differently, generally it stimulated a more thoughtful, a more cerebral side of a person, and that it was nothing like alcohol.

By the time I finished my reefer 101 lecture, Mae said that she would like to try some. By the time we had finished the first small bowl, Mae was laughing hysterically and falling off the bed. Layers of bone-weary tiredness fell off of me with her laughter, and soon we were both laughing deeply, and most likely, not about the same thing.

In the middle of one of my laughs, Mae pulled me down onto her and she made, or we made, the wildest love making I had ever experienced. I remember thinking as I slid off Mae's wet body and onto the cool, inviting sheets and starting to slip almost immediately into a coma, *What a perfect way to end such a strange day.*

*** *

This strange day still had some life left in the form of Mae getting the raging munchies. Never underestimate the power of the Thai lady with the raging munchies. Within half an hour, the disgruntled Peter was knocking at our door, with his hair standing up on the back of his head, waiting to "take us anywhere in Bangkok, twenty-four hours a day, first-class." As the sun came up in Bangkok, Mae and I were having a Thai breakfast in a cramped hole-in-the-wall restaurant, down a tiny alleyway in the heart of Bangkok. It was the beginning of a magical week with a wonderful Thai woman, who shared with me her body, her heart, and her family.

After our breakfast we went back to Mae's bar and paid for her to be with me the full week, which gave her great face among her peers. Mae told me later she would've lost face if Peter had returned her to the bar our first night. More so, had I exchanged her for another girl. So she stayed and hoped things would turn out all right. If you're happy with your girl and you keep her for more than one day, one of the traditions is to give her money to go have her hair done during the afternoon in preparation for your evening together. It gives a girl time to take the hair money and buy food for her family, see her children, and probably have her mother or sister fix her hair.

One afternoon I decided to skip the shopping trip with Peter and just go on a walk by myself. On my way back to the hotel to meet Mae, I stopped in at a little corner shop for a cold orange Nehi. When the shopkeeper delivered my soda, he asked me if I had a girl—or that's what I thought he said. And I said yes. I noticed that he went directly behind the curtain in the back room, and there was a lot of talking and people moving around. About the time I was finished drinking my soda and getting ready to go, the shopkeeper appeared from behind the curtain.

Following him was a little girl of probably eleven or twelve, with a clean dress and an unmistakable look of apprehension on her face, and what I assumed was the mother and then the grandmother following behind her. I realized that he was offering me his twelve-year-old daughter. I got flustered. And I said, "No, I told you I have a girl. I don't want any little girls," and I turned and walked out the door. As I walked out the door, my glance caught the look of disappointment on the faces of everyone. What I didn't understand at that moment was what I was seeing was the true face of poverty. *How poor do ya have to be for it to be okay to offer your twelve-year-old daughter to a stranger for sexual favors?*

Mae explained to me how the Thai people felt about the sex trade and the necessity for it. Sometimes the only way a family can survive is by sending one or two of their daughters into the sex trade. As I walked faster than usual back to the hotel, I thought about what a mistake I had made. I should have taken that little girl and bought her a nice meal, a beautiful dress, given her a few extra dollars, and taken her back home. I felt guilty about that incident for a long time.

Every day was different except that Mae and I would take a little reefer break a couple of times a day back to the room, make tender love sometimes, have lunch, and then have Peter take us some place new or exciting. It was his mission.

I spent a magical week with Mae, and I know I fell in love with her. We visited her grandmother in an elevated house way out in the country. I felt very privileged the several times we visited her father's house, built right on one of Bangkok's famous canals. From the outside, her father's house looked almost shabby, but once we stepped inside and removed our shoes, it was like this magical place. All of the wood in the house was dark and highly polished. I drank cold beer, laughed a lot, and played some kind of dominoes for very small amounts of money with Mae's father and grandfather. What a great time! I never won, and they just loved it.

Peter was true to his word and never let us down. And I definitely got my money's worth out of that guy. Mae always seemed to get the 3 a.m. munchies, and off we would go. Peter's hair standing up on the side and chain-smoking cigarettes, he drove us deep into Bangkok to places like a funky stall erected on the sidewalk, whose specialty was snake and noodles. The three of us sort of hit it off—one of those continual, high-intensity, good-vibe experiences. We packed a lot of adventures, incredible meals, honest laughter, and smiles into one week. We all knew what was coming.

The morning of my departure, I looked at Mae's sweet sleeping face on her pillow and knew this was the most in love I had ever been. I don't know how Mae really felt about me. We both shared our hearts in that week, and we also talked about the impossibilities of taking what we were feeling any further. I don't know why it's important, but I hope she remembers me.

26

During the time I was gone on R&R in Bangkok, the Marine Corps base and airfield in Danang had come under very heavy rocket and mortar attacks. The hospital had taken several direct hits. I worked my way through all the destruction back to the Third Marine Headquarters area, and I have a clear memory of the faces I was seeing. Most of the marines didn't have the look of complacent, behind-the-lines, office pogeys they'd had a week ago; the war had come to *their* backyard. No more ice-cold beer, steak cookouts, and movies in the outdoor theater. The shit was hitting the fan here, and they looked like it.

Rounding the corner of what was left of a large wing of the hospital, I ran into Doc Kristie, our old corpsman from F Company, 2nd Battalion, 3rd Marines. The last time I saw Doc Kristie was just a few minutes before we moved out on the big rescue operation in February that wiped out a lot of our battalion. Doc didn't get wounded then and went on to Okinawa with what was left of the company. He had a lot of details about what happened to everyone. The guys who were wounded in February were actually the lucky ones. The battalion rotated to Okinawa and filled in the missing ranks with new guys from the States. They all were introduced to the new plastic jungle rifle, the M-16 (the motherfucker from Mattel), and their accurate, dependable M-14s were put into a big warehouse.

The first operation—the first test of all the new, untested marines, with their new untested rifles—was to launch a major counterassault on the North Vietnamese Army dug in around Khe San. Hill 881 and Hill 861 had heavily fortified bunkers and tunnels filled with highly motivated NVA.

Doc confirmed what I had heard about the M-16. Unlike the M-14, the most reliable weapon I ever shot, the M-16 would jam—sometimes even if it was clean. Doc told me with tears in his eyes about Lance

Corporal Bean* who died with a bullet hole in his head and a jammed M-16. He told me of the bravery he had witnessed amongst our old friends. He saw Lance Corporal Phil Skinner** cut to pieces with machine gun fire trying to save some pinned-down marines. He also saw PFC Leonard Picanso get killed trying to take out a bunker.

I really liked Picanso—he was our FNG. On his first operation, the heat and the terrain kicked his ass, and he came down with heatstroke. They medevaced him out of the field and put him on permanent mess duty until we left for Okinawa. He was devastated; he had lost face. I gave him my sister's address and told him to write her. Vikki later told me he wrote her beautiful letters, containing thoughtful poetry.

Doc Kristie had definitely changed since the last time I'd seen him. We joined F Company about the same time. Doc Kristie was about 5 foot 8 or 9 inches, had short red hair, and tons of big reddish freckles. As our company corpsman, I felt he sometimes came off a little arrogant, a little too gung ho. I think in his heart, he would have rather been a combat marine than a navy corpsman. In hindsight Doc Kristie needed to prove something to himself a little more than the rest of us. He was the best corpsman I ever saw working with the wounded. A lot of grunts owe a lot to Doc Kristie. Doc had seen too much. And now he seemed in a slightly manic state; he needed to show me, and keep showing me, and keep telling me what had happened the night before.

The hospital had taken a direct hit, and a mortar hit a marine dead center. As Doc was going through the rubble back and forth, he would stop and pick up something and say in kind of an odd—distracted way— "Now see, see, shit, here's a piece of the guy right here—oh, shit."

Doc said early that morning he brought a body bag down and thought he had picked the entire guy up. Doc said the body bag had already been taken out somewhere to a cold-storage unit. Doc had spent the last half hour discovering how much of the guy he had missed. There were pieces of

---

* He was with Blevins and me when we were wounded
** My old gung ho buddy from boot camp

this marine embedded in the wood, and under boards, and in a blown-out filing cabinet—all over. Doc wanted to show me how much material was accumulating in his garbage can, and I didn't really need to look more than once. One or two little pieces were okay to throw away, but now he had collected more than just a few, and Doc didn't seem to know what to do with them. I suggested we get a solid plastic bag, put all of the pieces in it, and see if he could find a way for the bag to catch up with the owner.

While I helped Doc do a final cleanup, I told him about what had happened to Art Vigil and Tom Burkhardt. I also told him about my nightmare search for all of the parts of Art Vigil's body.

I had a helicopter to catch back to Camp Carroll. I turned and looked Doc Kristie in the eyes, him with his plastic bag of pieces of some marine unknown to me. What I saw in Doc Kristie's eyes, and he no doubt saw in mine, I am unable to explain—only that we were changed. We weren't the same, the rookie corpsman and the FNG grunt of a year ago. The look in Doc's eyes and mine were exactly the same, and we could understand all that we were seeing in each other. We shook hands and did about-faces. Doc had a bag to deliver, and I had a helicopter to catch. Within half an hour, I would find out that Vietnam was over for me.

The helicopter landed back at Camp Carroll, only for me to find Smitty pacing excitedly by the dusty LZ. Walt had a wonderful animated way about him. My orders had come to go home, and he was yelling that I could "start packing my shit immediately" and "your ass is out of here tomorrow."

It didn't take me long to pack up all my gear. That night they held a pretty good going-away party for me in the enlisted men's club tent. Tom Lazich and Walt Smith came down to see me off. I climbed into the waiting 4x4 for the final drive to Danang. They still had three or four months left in Vietnam, and I was going home.

I'm trying to remember how I felt about leaving Vietnam. I have a memory of flying out of Danang, looking out the airliner's window and seeing a patchwork of rice paddies, a bit of jungle-like shoreline, and then beautiful aquamarine-colored water. How could a peaceful-looking place of such intense outward beauty contain so much horror? So many memories, good and bad, and knowing I was leaving Vietnam *alive* caused painful waves of melancholy to well up in my chest. I wrote this poem in my notebook on the flight home.

Feeling the hate, pity and sorrow
Not really wanting to go out and fight
Wondering, if he will live to see tomorrow
Dying a thousand times, in the endless night.
Cradled in his arms, his only friend dies
Losing a part of himself when his friend is gone
The words still ringing, as he closes the sightless eyes
Please, don't let me die. Oh God, I want my mom.
Feeling the misery of the wind and rain
Fighting the heat and the never-ending mud
Finally breaking and crying from the pent-up pain
Holding the lifeless hand covered with blood.
Confusing hate for what is sorrow
Anxious, yet hesitant to go back and fight
Wondering if he will live to see tomorrow
Dying a thousand times in the endless night
War could not exist if we loved each other
As he loved the friend he called his brother.

27

Long before my plane touched down in America, I felt this growing sense of apprehension, not unlike the feeling that comes over you a couple of hours before a big operation. It was like there was some kind of danger waiting for me; I could feel it, but I didn't know what it was. Probably at this point, the scariest feeling was that I was not quite sure who I was now or how I was supposed to feel inside.

My dad had taken a job managing the Chamber of Commerce in Caldwell, Idaho, while I was in Vietnam. Again, I was going home to a place I'd never been. When my plane landed in Salt Lake City, I called my dad to give him a heads-up that I would be landing in Boise in a little over an hour. I told him not to tell Mom where she was going, just to load her up into the car for a drive. I always loved surprising my mom. Once our plane was in the air out of Salt Lake City, a middle-aged man in the front of the plane, wearing an expensive suit, sent me back a double Scotch and made a loud toast so everyone in the plane could hear him say, "Welcome back home, Marine." I did notice the stewardess looked at me differently for the rest of the flight—in a good way.

Surreal is the only word that comes to mind as I watched my family running to greet me when I stepped off the plane. The memory that stands out—besides hugging my mother—was the look on my little brother's face and how he looked at me.

"Well, that's more like it!" he said when I gave him a hug. When I had left a year earlier, he had teased me about having one little fire watch ribbon, and a PFC stripe.

It was mid-December in Idaho. I was close to hypothermia before they packed me into the family car to take me home for some of Mom's home cooking. On the ride to Caldwell, I kept feeling a sense of dread instead of well-being; I kept thinking that I hoped I would be okay and I wouldn't do anything to embarrass my family or myself. I kept reminding myself that in every one of the debriefing classes in Okinawa, the instructors reminded us several times that it may take "a few weeks to get adjusted to being stateside again."

I have little bits of memory of Christmas 1968. Grandpa and Grandma Lock came for Christmas. It was a nice Christmas, and Mom cooked a great meal. Everyone tried real hard to make me feel special, and while I appreciated their effort, I just wanted to be treated like they had always treated me. My mind kept drifting as we opened presents; I kept thinking that it had only been a year ago that I had been given a carton of cigarettes for Christmas by my first black Santa Claus.

All through my Christmas meal, I kept seeing Corporal Moses's face, as we pulled him down the streambed, the tiny, bloodless hole in his temple. After dinner my grandfather came down and sat on the end of the bed in my room and wanted to know if I was going to be all right. For my grandfather, a fundamentalist preacher, the way to deal with most of life's major problems was to pray.

"Bring your heart to the Lord, son." I assured my grandfather that everything was going to be okay, and I would make sure that I said a prayer every night, but I knew it was just saying words to make my grandfather happy. How could a loving God allow the pain and suffering and all the untold atrocities that happened in Vietnam? How could I say a prayer to God in gratitude or for forgiveness when I wanted to scream out all my anger and frustration?

All things considered, my twenty days of leave went without many significant incidents. I worked hard at forcing old memories from my mind. I think this was the first time in my life I started learning how to be in the moment, trying to force out the issues that were troubling me. When I least expected it, some graphic memory would just come into my head like a sucker punch from a barroom drunk. Many so vivid that I could almost hear and smell what I was remembering. I took walks with my mother, read to my little sister, played board games with my siblings and their friends, and avoided thinking or talking about Vietnam as much as possible. One evening just after Christmas, Donnie Hodge, my best friend from junior high school in Twin Falls, Idaho, called me from a local tavern in Caldwell. I don't remember exactly how he found out I was in town or even why he was in town. Donnie wanted me to join him and "get caught up on old times." I promised him I'd see him in an hour or so, but when it came time, I couldn't get myself to go out the front door. Part of me would have liked to have seen Donnie, but I just couldn't get myself to go out in public, especially in large crowds. The most significant "adjustment" incident that happened on leave again took me by total surprise. A new side of what I had been feeling revealed itself.

The plan was for my mom, Paul, my baby sister, Kris, and me to go up to visit my grandparents for New Year's Eve 1968 in Sweet, Idaho, about a two-hour drive from Caldwell. There was a light cover of fresh snow on the ground the morning we left. It was very cold but the sun was out, causing everything to sparkle under a bright, clear blue sky. I remember being excited because I was going to drive a car, I'd always been very passionate about driving, and it had been over a year since I had slid a key into an ignition. It was almost like music to hear a cold engine turn over and then fire up. I turned on the heat and watched the windshield defrost. I found a good radio station while Mom loaded my brother and little sister into a warm car. I settled in behind the wheel and "got on the road." What a good feeling— it felt so good, so normal.

I smoked a lot of cigarettes back then; I lit one up, and cracked my window when we came through Meridian, Idaho—a small farm town. At the same time as we rolled up to a stoplight, a bus or maybe a large truck, stopped in the lane next to me and hit his air brakes. With my window open, it must've sounded like incoming, because before I knew it, I had "hit the deck." My knee hit the accelerator, and we lurched several feet into the intersection before my mother grabbed the wheel and yelled my name. For that instant, I was trying to get down before a mortar round exploded next to me. I couldn't believe I did that—what the hell just happened? As my mom drove us on up to the grandparents in Sweet, I sat in the passenger seat and smoked cigarettes out the window. I kept thinking, "Well, there's no doubt about it now—I'm a hell of a long way from being okay."

28

Sometime in mid-January 1968, I reported to duty at company headquarters 2nd Battalion, 5th Marine Division, Camp Pendleton, California. Second Battalion, 5th Marines, was a new battalion in the making, and I was in the first group of marines to report to Headquarters Company. The sun was starting to go down as my group of half a dozen marines found a World War II–vintage Quonset hut that was F Company headquarters, located at the edge of a large parade deck. The Quonset was empty except for a couple of desks and a file cabinet at the front end. Behind one of the desks was a heavyset gunnery sergeant in charge of F Company headquarters, named Rodrigues. He had a pile of our service record books (SRB) on the desk in front of him. My first impression of "Gunny" was that he seemed wound a little too tight, with a big smile and humorless eyes. He himself had just reported in that morning. Without looking up, Sergeant Rodrigues barked out, "Nutting, which one of you assholes is Nutting?" He had seen in my SRB that I had taken a business course in civilian life and I knew how to type, so he drafted me as F Company's new unit diary clerk. By "drafted," I mean, his eyes locked on to me, he gave me one of his big toothy smiles, and said, "Says here you can type, so until I can find a real unit diary clerk, you are it, asshole, and you can start most ricky fuckin' ticky."

Taking on the unit diary was one of the toughest mental challenges that I had done in a very long time. I had to learn a special kind of shorthand code that kept track of every event and every marine, from who was on leave to who was AWOL in the company. Every entry had to be perfect. God help the unit diary clerk who turned their unit diary over to the captain for inspection with an incorrect code entry. The unit diary was six carbon-copy form sheets fastened together. There were no correcting typing errors either: you hit one wrong key and you started over. For the first two weeks, I don't think I left that Quonset hut except to go to the chow hall or to return from the captain's office with my rejected unit diary; staunch the bleeding from my severe ass-chewing, and start over yet again. At first, it was just a mind-boggling nightmare for me. After a couple of weeks, I did find I was enjoying the challenge quite a bit, because I was getting better at it and it really did give me time to think about little else. As long as I looked at myself as a grunt, just temporarily filling in as an office pogue, I could handle this for a while.

One of the biggest incentives for me to stay on this unit diary job and out of the barracks was this: 28th Marines was a transition battalion. Marines who were not yet eighteen years old went to 28th Marines; you can't legally die for your country until you are eighteen. Many of the returning Vietnam veterans were marines who had less than a year to do and were waiting to muster out. We also had many medical and mental marines working on some type of discharge.

For the marines in the barracks, it was just the same old stuff day after day. Inspections, close order drill, physical training, and more inspections, and there were always overnight field operations going on.* The idea was to take all these "old salts" and put them with the boot marines and teach them everything they needed to know about how to stay alive in Vietnam. Humping up and down the steep hills of Camp Pendleton in the middle of the night, shooting blanks, and teaching some seventeen-year-old the best way to kill another human was just about the last thing I wanted to do.

The challenge of the unit diary made the hours and days fly by; I lived for the weekends. Starting from around 1700 Friday afternoon until 0530 Monday morning were my precious hours that I didn't have to be a marine at all. I had an exciting new girlfriend who was rich and was ready for almost anything as long as it was "far out."

This was 1968 in Southern California. The United States was in turmoil. People were protesting in the streets with peace marches to end the war. There were race riots in Watts, the hippie movement, communal living, free love, the Height Ashbury, Whisky a Go-Go, Pacific Palisades,

---

* War games

the Black Panthers, and the Symbionese Liberation Army, the Beatles, the Rolling Stones, Janis Joplin, Jimi Hendrix, and the assassinations of Bobby Kennedy and Martin Luther King Jr. College professor and LSD Guru Timothy Leary was urging everyone to "tune in, turn on, and drop out." LSD could be found anywhere—every club or street corner.

From Venice Beach and the more laid-back surfer scene to the bright lights and glitter of Hollywood and the Sunset Strip, everywhere vibrated with an electric energy you could almost feel on your skin. True hippies and wannabes, stoners and bikers and the curious, whoever they may be, it seemed they all had one or two very common threads: to go on some kind of "trip" or at least get as high as possible, and then if you were lucky you would experience some kind of liberated free love with a liberated flower child. This was the time of go-go boots and extreme miniskirts; women were burning their bras. Besides everything else going on in America, there was a real sexual revolution happening. Everything was happening at once, from music to politics, and every moment of free time I spent away from the Marine Corps, I felt in some way I was looking for peace within myself, chemically, mentally, spiritually, and physically.

It's hard to explain the exhilarating surge that I felt each time I nodded at the guard on Friday afternoon, as he waved me through the back gates of Camp Pendleton.

I tried to make every weekend a new adventure: rock concerts, camping trips, scuba diving, or even investigating Scientology. It was all out there, just outside the gate.

The answer just had to be out there. Maybe the elimination of nightmares and bad thoughts were just as easy as taking a pill, or attending long Scientology confrontational sessions with another person "to become clear," or the surefire method of sliding into oblivion after too much wine and reefer.

Many weekends I would head up to Hollywood, up Tiger Tail Road. I had an open invitation to come visit the Lazich family. Tom Lazich had rotated out of the Marines and was living at home. Tom and his siblings were born with silver spoons in their mouths.

Tom's father, Brontaslave, was a top ophthalmologist in Hollywood. Tom grew up around Hollywood stars and their children. He claimed Jerry Mather, the star of *Leave it to Beaver*, was his friend and baseball teammate. Tom's mother was a gourmet cook and a stoned alcoholic. Tom had an older brother, Michael, who was still in the Marine Corps. He had two sisters—one off at college—and a hot younger sister, Susie, who, after three or four weekend visits, fell madly in love with me for a short period of time.

I was always guaranteed a great weekend when I visited the Lazich family. They lived in a large house that was way more upscale than anything I was used to. There were always exotic cocktails, fine wines, and gourmet meals. Susie was into the hipster scene big-time. Money never seemed to be an object, and during the time that I was dating Susie, she had an apartment on Venice Beach before she moving to an even hipper apartment off the boardwalk in San Diego. Tom was dating Susie's very liberated best friend, Vikki. At first, coming back to a world of free love and sexual liberation was almost unbelievable to me. There were many catchphrases for the time, and Vikki's motto was, "If it feels good, do it." Vikki was an equestrian with a couple of very expensive thoroughbreds. Several times, Tom, Susie, and I smoked reefer in the grandstands while Vikki cantered her horse around the ring until she had "several far-out climaxes." Whatever we wanted to do, we just did it. I had just survived thirteen months on the DMZ, and I was back in the world. Bring it on. There were great parties on Venice Beach or seeing top bands like Ike and Tina Turner at the Pacific Palisades, or Charlie Musselwhite at the Whisky a Go-Go. On the way in to a rock concert to see Jimi Hendrix, I observed two couples vigorously copulating between a line of chrome-covered choppers, and nobody paid much attention. Everything felt so different.

29

What I did on the weekends was my business. All through the work-week, I took being a marine very seriously. My uniform was squared away, and I always had a nice spit shine on my shoes. I consistently had high proficiency and conduct marks. For my work on the unit diary, I was promoted to corporal and given a three-day pass for going an entire week without any errors.

This was springtime of 1968, and I had an appointment at the base's main hospital to X-ray some shrapnel that was still in my leg. The road was closed through the base because of construction, so in order to make my appointment at the hospital, I had to drive my car out the San Clemente exit and onto the freeway and come in through the main entrance at Oceanside. While I was signing out of the company office, there was some shitbird sitting next to the door. He was getting mustered out of the Marines due to a psychiatric evaluation and had an appointment at the hospital around the same time I did.

The first sergeant said, "Nutting, you'd love to give this asshole a ride to the hospital, wouldn't you?" I said sure, and a few minutes later we were picking up speed down the I-5 freeway. The PFC sitting next to me never shut up; from the minute he shut the car door, a steady stream of words came out of his mouth. I offered him a cigarette as I rolled down my window and let the rush of warm California air drown out my mouthy passenger. In hindsight, I know we talked a little about being in Vietnam, if we had smoked pot or seen much combat; at the most I was only half listening to the guy. He was explaining to me all the reasons that he was getting out on a psychiatric discharge. About that same time he shook out a regular-looking piece of Chiclet gum from a small box, popped it in his mouth, and offered me one. I took one and started chewing thinking it was because we were smoking cigarettes, until he said, "You just wait,"

"What do you mean?" I asked.

"You said that you got high, didn't ya? That's fuckin' first-class LSD in that gum. I chew it and then I go talk to the fuckin' psychiatrists. Those fuckers just think I am so fuckin' nuts."

I had chewed that psychedelic Chiclet for no more than twenty seconds before I spit it out the window. I immediately felt panic and extreme anger. I wanted to push the son of a bitch out the door while we were still going seventy miles per hour. My mind was racing. I decided maybe chewing it only twenty seconds had only given me a small dose, and if I concentrated real hard, maybe I could fake my way through this appointment. Before I had time to decide on how I was going to inflict some kind of retribution on the flake next to me, we were being waved through by the guard at the main gate of Camp Pendleton. About a hundred yards into the base, I stopped my car and told this sorry ass, poor excuse for a marine to get out, and the next time I saw him, I was going to seriously fuck him up.

I still felt okay when I pulled my car into the hospital parking lot. I thought maybe everything was going to be all right, maybe the guy was just kidding me, and maybe it was just a plain piece of gum; psycho fuckers can be like that. When I locked up my car and looked around, I thought I felt a little different. Objects around me appeared to have slightly shifted from my perspective. Walking across the parking lot, I felt a tightening in my chest, and it seemed like my heart was racing. I had a fleeting hopeful thought that maybe this was real weak stuff, and if my situation didn't get much worse, I would be able to get past whatever effect it had on me.

Camp Pendleton's main hospital was a series of buildings and Quonset huts connected by several wide main corridors and many interconnecting hallways. The minute I stepped inside the hospital, I knew I was in trouble. The main entrance, with its highly polished linoleum floor seemed to go on and on into infinity. It seemed that every step I took toward the X-ray department, I got a little higher; I could physically feel it. I felt almost an overwhelming sense of paranoia as I walked past any officer or doctor. I felt as if everyone could see that I was totally tripped out. *Oh shit*, I was thinking, *I can't let on that I am freaking out inside.*

As I passed people in the endless hallway, their faces didn't look right—almost sinister. I tried to avoid so many people in the main corridor by turning down a side hallway, only to make eye contact with a double amputee, and then around the corner, a guy on a gurney with all the tubes and bags hanging out of him. I felt like running out of there screaming, but by that time I wasn't really sure which direction I needed to go. Maybe an hour and an eternity of weird shit went by before I finally made it to the X-ray department. By that time I was unable to speak. I handed my orders to the corpsman behind the desk, but every time I tried to say something, the words just died in my throat, and only a raspy squeak would come out. He must've figured I was just another one of those totally messed-up Vietnam veterans. He told me I was late for my appointment. He said he didn't have time to do what he needed to do before noon chow. He said to come back at 1300, and he wrote me out a chit for the mess hall. I think the last thing I really wanted to do was eat, but that's where I was told to go, so I went. Shuffling through the chow line, they piled unwanted food on my tray.

I felt unable to tell them that I didn't want it. I felt everyone in the mess hall must know I was high on LSD and that I could flip out and my head could explode at any moment. The chicken leg and the mashed potatoes and gravy looked like they were moving on their own in my tray. When I tried to get my coffee cup up to my lips, my hands shook so bad that I spilled coffee down my utility shirt. I left my full tray of food on the table and bolted for the door to the outside. I heard someone yell behind me about policing up my shit as I headed outside. I never turned around. I just kept walking until I found a tree away from most of the activity, and there I sat for the rest of the afternoon, fighting down periodic waves of panic and thinking of ways to pay back the asshole who did this to me. He must've mustered out soon after the LSD incident, because I never saw him again. In hindsight, I never tried all that hard to find him.

30

I never cared much for Sergeant Rodrigues, our company's first sergeant. He had this artificial smile when he told me what a great job I was doing on the unit diary. He took personal pride in his unit diary, and it gave him bragging rights among the other company sergeants down at the enlisted men's club. As long as I did my job and had a perfect unit diary, he left me alone most of the time. I even earned a few three-day weekends and many pats on the back, but I always felt he was the kind of guy who would leave your ass hanging out to dry if he felt his was on the line.

Rodrigues had that same smile when he was highly pissed off; only his eyes took on a real cold look. Anytime I didn't totally agree with him one hundred percent, he would take on this crazy smile, and through his teeth he would always make the same threat, something like, "Listen, Nutting, you don't like the way I do it, you can go back to being a fucking grunt. You wanna stand all those inspections; you wanna go humping around all those fuckin' hills, you wanna do field ops on the weekend? That's the land of port and starboard liberty, asshole—think it over." I didn't do much thinking about it before it finally happened.

Rodrigues was being a particular jerk one day and made his threat about me going back to the "land of the grunts," when I stood up from behind my desk and said something like, "Well, hell, Sergeant Rodrigues, that's a whole lot better than working for someone like you, so I'll be packing up my shit now and be heading into the barracks." Sergeant Rodrigues didn't say one word right then, but I could see that he was livid as I walked out of company headquarters carrying out my threat.

At that time I didn't realize what kind of enemy I had made. Rodrigues hated me; that's what my fellow office pogeys related to me later on, anyway. Good old Sergeant Rodrigues was spending some real late nights with my replacement working on the unit diary, and he was not a happy man.

As for life out in the barracks as a grunt, I found that daily inspections, drill, formations, and physical training were far better than being under the thumb of Gunny Rodrigues. I was given a squad of seventeen-year-olds and shitbirds, which turned out to be one of the most satisfying jobs I had in the Marine Corps. Out in the field, I tried to teach them things to be aware of in combat and how to stay alive. I liked most every one of those kids in my squad, and I could tell they appreciated me. There would be times on some field operations and where we'd break for chow, or have a smoke, we would talk about things the Marine Corps didn't teach them.

The Corps had taught them everything it could about staying alive and protecting fellow marines in combat. The Marine Corps taught them how to kill another human being. What it didn't teach every crop of fresh-faced seventeen- and eighteen-year-old privates headed to Vietnam was that you also had to protect your soul and your humanity. Coming out of boot camp, marines know that they may have no other choice but to take another human life to protect themselves and their fellow marines. Killing an enemy is not something to take pride in, only doing the very best job you can in a combat situation. The minute a marine or any combatant carves their initials into a dead enemy's forehead, cuts their ear off to wear around their neck on a bootlace, or knocks out their gold teeth for a "groovy souvenir," they step past the point of no return. You can't commit an atrocity to a fallen enemy, or some form of cruelty to a Vietnamese peasant, and expect to come home and live a normal life. I told them a few stories about Corporal Rhodes—basically a real nice guy and a good marine, who let the hatred of an enemy and a race of people change him so radically that the only place he felt he fit in in this life was "on the DMZ killing gooks."

August 1, 1968*

My dearest family,

I apologize for my childish actions in the past few weeks.** It's just that some-times I get so low, so discouraged, so disappointed in myself and in the people that constantly surround me. I just want to chuck it all. The military is such a suppressive organization that sometimes things get almost unbearable. It's not that I am a quitter or that I can't hack what they dish out, but it is so hard to be made to do something you know is wrong, or don't believe in. I have such a desire to become myself and be the person I want to be. It only makes me feel worse when I realize that I am letting trivial matters mount up and get under my skin. I guess no matter how mature a man is, he needs a shoulder to cry on. Don't worry about me, I'll be okay, and with each day I'll just be one day closer to my goal. I am searching for something in life. I know it'll take a long period of time before I'm able to achieve my goal. Life is just too short for a man to get all he wants out of it. It doesn't matter what a man does in his short life, as long as he is happy and finds what he is looking for. The time came when I broke away from the womb completely and I have achieved this fairly well. I consider my parents more like very close friends than parents. Someone I can turn to under any circumstances and know I'll never be rejected. I guess no matter how long I live all always have that desire to be a little boy again, and just live with my family just as I always have. Now as a man I realize I must find my place in life, which I always cast doubt when I look at it. Looking at life is a big challenge, but I am eager to start. You won't be getting any more bummer phone calls. No matter how eloquent my vocabulary is, or how articulate I am, I'll never be able to express the love I have for my family. Don't worry-remember, I am a Nutting, and they can knock us down, but we won't stay there for long.

Love,
John

---

* Just a few weeks before my twenty-first birthday
** I'm probably referring to how I became a grunt again

31

September 1968 started out with great promise. It was Labor Day weekend, and I had a three-day pass. Tom, Mike, and Susie Lazich had been planning a Labor Day blowout in Mexico for a couple of weeks. Around the first part of August, I met an East Coast "flower child" named Katherine, with dark hair eyes, from the Boston area. She shared an apartment with her sister that was above Tom and Mike's apartment. We met at one of the Lazich boy's weekend barbecues, and it seemed like the minute our eyes made contact there was an instant chemistry, and I was eager to spend more time with her. That was my choice, spend a passionate, quiet weekend with a beautiful new love interest, or go to Ensenada with the Lazich brothers and all their high school friends, plus all of Susie's entourage.

Sometimes, it's those seemingly insignificant decisions that end up taking your life in totally unexpected directions. I think what ended up swaying my decision was not only howling at the moon in Mexico with my old brothers, but they had rented a private beach out of Ensenada with its own security and it had a "'totally bitchin' rock jetty that goes way the fuck out into the ocean." I just couldn't pass it up, so I went.

I only remember parts of that evening, but what I do remember is this: we went to a very popular bar, I think its name was Hussong's. I have never been in a bar, or any room for that matter, with so many people packed inside. There were people under tables trying to avoid whatever was flying through the air at the moment. Every square inch of the overflow benches had someone standing on it, making it seem like people were stacked up against the walls. By midnight, everyone was thoroughly saturated with gallons of Mexican beer and shots of cheap tequila. We were close to exhaustion after hours of dancing to an ear-splitting Mexican cowboy band, when our following migrated to the beach for the bonfire and sleeping bag phase.

It seemed like everybody wanted to participate in adding driftwood to the fire, and in no time, the bonfire was five or six feet high.

After an hour around the burning shrine of heaping driftwood, staring into the growing flames, feeling the heat on my face, and looking through the bonfire flames at all the illuminated, animated, psychedelic, and incapacitated faces, I needed some space; so I got up and slipped away unnoticed. Crossing the beach to the jetty, I noticed how exceptionally clear and bright the stars were, and a sense of contentment washed over me. The world was no longer tilting, as the alcohol was wearing off, and the half-dozen or so hits of reefer that I had had around the campfire wrapped me in a blanket of mellowness. I found a configuration of rocks toward the end of the jetty that I could somewhat comfortably stretch out on like a caveman lounge chair, so I could see the panorama of extremely bright stars above me. I remember listening to the waves beating its rhythm against the rocks, looking into the stars and letting my mind soar into the universe.

I must have soared right into unconsciousness, because sometime in the middle of the night, maybe three or four in the morning, I had a very sobering feeling that my right elbow was on fire. My first waking thought was that I had fallen asleep by the campfire, but as soon as the cobwebs cleared, I knew I'd been bitten by something. The few minutes I sat on the rock thinking about what to do next, the pain seemed to intensify about tenfold.

I knew I was in trouble, and I headed back to the camp. A very painful pouch was starting to form on my elbow. The only people awake at that time were the people who had taken psychedelics, and they were hallucinating. The only response I got from them was: "Look, look at that. Wow! Far out!" One chick got "freaked out" and went running up the beach until her boyfriend caught her, and several others thought it was "totally fucking hysterical" and kept asking me to "show us your elbow, man."

It took until several hours after dawn before anyone was sober enough even to consider driving back to the states. It was midday by the time the Lazich boys got me across the border and to Camp Pendleton's hospital emergency room. By that time the poison had spread, I was almost delirious, and my elbow looked like it had an angry red apple growing off the end.

I was very sick for a couple of days—feverish episodes of weird dreams and fuzzy realities. I do remember whoever was taking care of me was quite impressed by my extremely high white blood cell count.

It took about a week for the swelling to go down and for me to start feeling like my old self. About that time, a couple of the marines in my squad came to visit me. I liked them both, even though they were a couple of real shitbirds. Lance Corporal Jasper had been a grunt rifleman in Vietnam and had been wounded; he had less than two months left on his enlistment. Jasper had been busted for pot in San Diego and had gone AWOL a couple of times since returning stateside. After Vietnam, Jasper would just as soon tell an officer to go fuck himself than salute him. Jasper was a local boy from Newport Beach and was part of the local surfer scene. I had gone on liberty with him a few times and met some of his old friends. Like I said, even though Jasper was a Marine Corps shit-bird, he was an okay guy.

Private Ing was a very young-acting, blond, bucktoothed seventeen-year-old from New York City who thought Jasper was the best thing since the Beach Boys. Private Ing loved any attention Jasper showed him, especially if Jasper talked to him about surfing. So anyway, Jasper and Ing were standing around my rack making small talk when Jasper cut to the chase.

I had left my car parked down in the battalion parking lot before I headed out for my weekend in Ensenada. Jasper wanted to borrow it. He said he could deliver it to the hospital parking lot the day I checked out. He said one of his old schoolmates had scored a large quantity of excellent reefer and was selling righteous, three-fingered baggies for ten dollars, but he needed to get on it because it was going fast.

Many times I've wondered why I made the decision I did that day; maybe I was pleased someone with a familiar face had come to visit me. Jasper did have a convincing style. Somehow the idea that I wasn't using my car right then, and it would be waiting for me just outside in the parking lot the day I got out, combined with the offer that I would receive an extra-large baggie of excellent Mexican weed, plus a full tank of gas, prompted me to hand my car keys over to Lance Corporal Jasper, and say, as they beat a hasty retreat out of my room, "You guys be careful."

September 12, 1968, was a beautiful sunshiny day, and after eleven days in Camp Pendleton hospital, I was finally checking out. Beams of sunlight streamed in the windows, reflecting brightly off the highly polished lino-leum of the hospital corridor as I went from one department to another. I couldn't help thinking that only a month ago, when I walked down the same corridors, I had experienced extreme fear and paranoia. Today I was feeling great. My elbow no longer hurt and looked almost normal, and most importantly I was getting the hell out of the hospital.

I almost laughed at my feeling of *déjà vu* when a few minutes before noon the pharmacy clerk told me that I couldn't check out of anymore places until 1300—after noon chow. On the way back to my room I spotted Lance Corporal Jasper and PFC Ing coming down the long hallway. They seemed excited and gave me a far-off greeting with waves and smiles. When we met up, Jasper said, "Well, ah, I've got some good news for ya and I've got some bad news for ya." I told him to tell me the bad news first, and he answered by telling me that he had gotten into a fender bender on the freeway, and some four-eyed geek had put a dent in my right front fender. It was the other guy's fault, there was a police report, and the guy had insurance.

Jasper told me the good news was that they had scored three fat lids, and one of those beauties was mine. I remember not feeling too upset about my car because the guy did have insurance, and I had a large bag of reefer. Katherine, the girl that I was seeing at the time, was kind of a fringe hippie. She did have a good-paying job and a nice apartment. Katherine loved to smoke reefer and snuggle in close. I was extremely anxious to see her. Every day in the hospital, I regretted choosing Ensenada over spending the weekend with her. Now the thought of bringing Katherine a big bag of reefer made my heart beat faster.

I had an hour until I could continue checking out of the hospital, so I suggested we go check out the damage to the fender of my beloved 1961 Ford Fairlane. The bright sunlight caused me to squint my eyes almost shut as I stepped outside for the first time in almost two weeks. When we crossed the parking lot I could feel the heat radiating through my thin hospital-issue slippers. It was not unusual to see marines going from one area to another in their hospital scrub pajamas and blue and white pinstripe bathrobes. Before we even got across the hot surface of the parking lot, I could see that the dent was much less than I had imagined. It was no big deal; it was a dent about as round as a basketball and deep enough that it had cracked the paint along the sharp edges. Later, I bought three "hippie flower power" stickers for a couple of dollars that covered the dent nicely, and they stayed on the car as long as I had it.

I wanted to get off the parking lot tarmac and onto some grass with shade. Jasper suggested that since we had an hour to kill, we ought to go down the by lake and try some of our newly acquired pot. I told him I wasn't into getting stoned anywhere near the hospital, but I would like to see the lake and sit in some shade.

Along the edge of the parking lot was a stand of trees and brush with a small trail that led down to a large man-made lake. Between the trees and the lake was a wide path. Jasper had started down the small trail ahead of Ing and me and had a chance meeting with two brig rats and a brig chaser on the main trail—old friends from his past. Ing and I hung back until they moved on. Later we sat in a small clearing with our feet at the edge of the path. Jasper was telling me the details of the car wreck when he pulled a joint from his utility-shirt pocket and lit it up with his trusty Zippo lighter. It was his Vietnam good luck Zippo, and he would nervously click the top open and shut, especially if he got excited. I was sitting in the middle, listening to Jasper's animated tale and smoking a cigarette. One time as I passed the joint between Jasper and Ing, I took a small puff just to taste the quality of our acquisition. Immediately after passing the joint to Ing, I spotted a woman walking down the main trail, coming our way. I took the joint out of Ing's hand, snubbed it out in the grass, and put the roach in my pocket. I gave the roach back to Jasper after the woman disappeared down the trail. Jasper clicked his Zippo once again and a large yellow-orange flame erupted from its windscreen. He put the crumpled end of the roach into the flame and puffed two or three times to give it a good start. Simultaneously, a shore patrolman jumped down out of the bushes in front of Jasper with his .45 caliber pistol drawn and said, "Give me that! You are under arrest."

I was placed in handcuffs, put in the back of a military police squad car, and taken to the Office of Naval Intelligence headquarters to be interviewed. The agent who interviewed me didn't really know what to think. He kept looking in my mouth and down my throat and in my eyes, but there was no obvious sign that I was high. I wasn't "freaking out" or acting in any way abnormal. They couldn't arrest us for being high since we didn't act unusual in any way. When they searched my pockets, they found my car keys. I signed a paper allowing them to search my car. In it they found one large baggie of marijuana in the glove compartment and some debris on the seats. The agents decided that before they could really file any charges, they had to find out what the green vegetable matter really was. By late afternoon, Jasper, Ing, and I were chauffeured back to the company area in a military sedan by two men in suits with high and tight haircuts. The "suits" went through our foot lockers and wall lockers, confiscating most of the contents, and then turned us over to our commanding officer.

32

Since no charges had been filed against me, I don't think command knew what to do with me. They weren't sure that the "green vegetation" was even marijuana, and whatever lab did the tests took an extremely long time confirming that it was. My life was in limbo. I was no longer part of the grunt company. No squad, no inspections, no war games; all I had to do was be present for the morning, afternoon, and evening formations.

I had full liberty, and my liberty was never restricted, even after the lab report came back positive for marijuana. I spent many hours between formations and liberty driving out to a deserted beach along the Camp Pendleton coastline, just to think about the situation I was in. Basically, I was in deep shit. My two choices were, I could go to Canada, or I could stand a general court-martial. At the time, the penalty for possession of marijuana on a military base was being busted down to private, given a bad-conduct discharge, and seven to ten years of hard time at Leavenworth Federal Prison.

It was hard for me to understand that after thirteen months in Vietnam at the request of my government, who wanted me to kill as many of the enemy as possible, would send me to prison for what amounted to taking one small puff of marijuana. I had a lot more time to think about it than I ever imagined, and eventually, almost six months passed before my court-martial convened.

About two weeks after we were arrested, PFC Ing went AWOL, and I never saw him again. I always wondered what happened to him.

It seemed like my only option was to get a good lawyer and try to figure out some answers to the mess I was in. I would sit in my car, parked on a bluff overlooking a deserted beach, drink a thermos of mess hall coffee, smoke endless cigarettes, and write down detailed answers to every question that I could think of. I focused in and prepared myself mentally; I played scenarios in my head almost to the point of meditation.

Day-to-day life on base was a constant struggle to stay focused and not panic inside. Almost every weekend I would spend with Katherine, just hanging out in her apartment, taking long walks, or having dinner at a new restaurant. It didn't matter because I knew that eventually we would smoke a little reefer, and then Katherine would take me to her bed and make me forget about everything.

In the six months I waited, my trial date was postponed twice. It was hell getting all psyched up and then being told it was delayed for three weeks or a month. As it turned out, I was the only one of the three of us to go on trial. In the time it took for the lab to come back with the marijuana verification, Lance Corporal Jasper's medical discharge came through, and he was mustered out of the Marine Corps. The government wasn't going to file charges against Jasper since he was a civilian. It was a matter of record that Jasper had been arrested before for marijuana possession.

An event that played well for me during this time was that shore patrolman HM3 Shaw, who made the initial arrests, had mustered out of the navy. He was a rookie patrolman with the Los Angeles police department. He couldn't take time off from his new job to come and testify at my trial and could only submit his written statement.

Just before my court-martial actually took place, I cracked a little. A week before, my trial date had been postponed yet again. It was in the wee hours of Monday morning, the weekend had been just outstanding, and Katherine was being particularly seductive. I had to leave her apartment by 3:30 a.m. to get back to base on time. Before I knew it, it was 3:45 a.m., and then 4:15 a.m., then 5 a.m., then . . . fuck it. I'm probably going to prison for seven years anyway, why do I want to leave the arms of this sensuous woman? This was the first blemish on my service record book.

February 24, 1969

My Dearest Family and Swede*,

Today I'm feeling very lonesome, and all I've thought about is being home. I looked through my album and read several old letters. Thursday I went before the company commander for being UA (unauthorized absence). He said I was a good man. Then he said he was on my side about the court-martial, and then he continued to give me an almost father-to-son lecture. Since I pleaded guilty to the UA, he said he would have to give me some kind of punishment, so I am on restriction for seven days. I feel very lucky because last week the Marine who went before him for eight hours UA received a bust, a $50 fine, and 30 days restriction. Plus it won't be entered into my record book until after the court-martial, because division legal won't let them have it. I have been in contact with Uncle Dick**, several times in the last two weeks. The last time he was at my defense counsel's office. He was trying to get all the information he could about the case. He said he wished he had known about it sooner, and it was just too late to even try and stop it. I explained that it is hard for me to ask for help, and I was a little embarrassed about the charges. He chuckled and said that it sounded like a typical Nutting trait, and that another trait is to help kin in need. If he can't do anything else, he has given me a little morale, and a buildup of my very low ego. He is a good man. My court-martial is going to be the 3rd or 4th of March, and although my chances of skating are practically nil, it no longer worries me. I have prepared myself both mentally and physically for the worst. The biggest bummer is that I would have been getting out on the first of March (seven days from now). I pray for the best. Since I have nothing but spare time while on restriction, I have been doing a lot of work on my book. Working on several new poems, and revising old ones. Well, Swede, I told you that you would feel at home around my family. They are good people and I miss them a lot. Our apartment and bikes (at least mine) may have to wait a while. For me, I'll probably have to spend some brig time.

Uncle Don, I have no words of advice for a man who leads a life that any male between 16 and 90 would be envious of. Both Tom and I had a very good time

---

*   Swede was out of the Marine Corps at this time living with my parents, staying in my old room.

**   My uncle was a retired Marine Corps colonel

talking with you.* he talked a lot about you when we got back. Rarely do I or Tom have the opportunity or want to get into a heavy rap about life and new ideas with anyone outside the younger crowd (not implying anything). But it was good to talk with someone of your age group who is on board with life, and is willing to listen and at least try and understand, you know an old duffer who hasn't let the years prejudice his mind. It's time to eat, so I'll end one of my seldom written letters. Take care and God bless.

Your son, brother, nephew and friend,

John

---

* This was during Christmastime, 1968, Caldwell, Idaho

33

By the time my trial date came, I was relieved just to get it over with, whatever the outcome. I had gone over many times the questions my lawyer was going to ask me. My assigned lawyer, Second Lieutenant Ralph L. Williams, used the outline that I had written to make much of his case. I was more than a little worried about him now that it was roughly two months before trial and I had only visited with him for maybe a couple of hours total. He'd been in the military a matter of months, probably just fresh out of college, and this was his first trial. He couldn't believe the powers that be had appointed him defense counsel in a general court-martial trial, and like I said, I had my doubts.

I stood in the barracks' head that fateful morning, looking in the mirror. My uniform was class A, inspection ready. I had a nice high and tight haircut. The night before, most of the guys in my squad were there in the barracks, showing their support for me. A young PFC known for his spit shine put one of his best on my shoes. When he gave them back to me he said, "Smile, Corporal Nutting, and you can see the cracks of your teeth in the reflection on the toes."

I looked at my reflection in the mirror one last time, adjusted my tie, and here we go. I had the same feeling just before a patrol. I remember taking a deep breath, squaring my shoulders, and walking out of the barracks to a waiting jeep and my "brig chaser," PFC Delgado. Delgado was a young, squared-away, gung ho, well-built Chicano marine from my squad whom I liked. The night before he had taken me aside and told me how very unhappy he was about his assignment as my brig chaser. In a whispery voice Delgado said, with a dead-serious face, screwed up with intensity and only inches away from mine, that if the court-martial went against me and they gave me hard time, it would be okay with him if I wanted to make a break for it.

Delgado, with his sincere look, told me several times that it was important for me to knock him out cold, and I had to "make it look really good." The look on his face was almost comical, but the whole situation was way too serious to be funny. Making a break for it at this point was something I never would have considered. But it was nice to know the guy three paces behind me, with a billy club and a .45 caliber pistol, considered me his friend.

I continuously smoked cigarettes for the thirty-minute jeep ride from Camp San Onofre to the main Camp Pendleton headquarters. Walking into the main judicial building, with Delgado right behind me, was like one of those real uncomfortable moments out of a weird dream. Our heels struck in unison, the sharp sound bouncing off the bulkheads, as we walked down the hall to the courtroom. Heads emerged from doorways; eyes followed us down the hall.

Soon it seemed the only sound in the building was our footsteps, as people silently stopped whatever they were doing and looked up from their desks. I had that old ambush feeling; I had stepped in far deeper shit than expected. I kept thinking, for some reason, this court-martial was being made into a very big deal. Why did the government decide to take the time and expense to mount a general court-martial case as big as this for minor marijuana possession?

I sat in the hallway waiting to go into the courtroom, wondering if some of this stemmed from my letters being put into the Congressional Record, including the comments about the incompetency from McNamara on down, about the Starlight scopes, and the wasting of lives on both sides fighting to take the same area time after time. It was just a fleeting thought, vanishing within a scant minute as the doors opened and I was ushered in.

I stood ramrod straight as my panel of judges, filed into the courtroom and took their seats. My gut sort of turned to liquid, my heart was racing, and my tongue kept sticking to the roof of my mouth, but I remembered to lock my squirrely eyeballs to the front, dig my thumbs into the seams of my trousers, and stand at attention until they were seated. Just being in the same room with this many officers would make most enlisted men pucker up a little tighter.

But what made it hard to suppress my initial paranoia of being hung out to dry was that once I took my seat, I noticed that Second Lieutenant Williams had been promoted to Captain! I remember thinking at the time, how did this guy get promoted two grades in rank in five days without ever trying a case, unless the powers that be felt it didn't look good for a second lieutenant to be the sole defense counsel on a general court-martial trial.

34

My court-martial convened on the morning of 24 March 1969. The court was called to order by Law Officer, Colonel William W. Wander, USMC.

The hardest part of the court-martial for me was the very start. Seated to my left behind a long elevated, dark-wood desk were one full-bird colonel, four lieutenant colonels, one major, and three captains. It seemed like I could physically feel their eyes boring into me, trying to get an early read of my guilt or innocence. I remember making myself look into each one's eyes and holding his gaze momentarily before looking at the next face, and thinking that this person has the power to bust me down to private, give me a dishonorable discharge, and send me to Leavenworth prison.

The first two witnesses were the special agents for the office of naval intelligence, Douglas R. Laird and George Carpenter, who had interrogated me and then ransacked my wall and footlockers back in September. They both looked like characters out of a Mickey Spillane novel, with off-the-rack suits and fresh buzz cuts. About the only thing informative that came from their testimonies was that the vegetable residue found in the pocket of my brown sport jacket they confiscated from my locker was so miniscule it could not be weighed. Even though my ass was on the line I couldn't help but appreciate the appearance of the two stereotypical special agents.

The trial was then adjourned for one-half hour. With Delgado hot on my heels, I had a few minutes to go to the head and then exit a side door and have a smoke outside. It was a beautiful spring morning, still a few weeks away until the Southern California sun baked all the moisture out of the plant life.

Outside, Delgado and I didn't say much, he just stood there with his eyes squinting from the bright light and had the same screwed-up worried look on his face he'd had in the squad bay the night before. At that moment I wasn't feeling so confident either. I was afraid of the fear starting to rise up inside me. I did not want to lie under oath. I remember thinking as I lit my second cigarette, this could be my last cigarette as a free man for a long time.

Upon the trial resuming, Williams made a motion to have my case thrown out due to lack of a speedy trial. My court-martial trial date had drug on so long that shore patrolman Shaw had mustered out of the navy and joined the Los Angeles Sheriffs Department. The petition was dismissed. The prosecution continued by submitting a written statement from their key witness, Shore Patrolman Shaw.

I was the next up to testify.

I had to stretch the truth. I don't think it would have mattered to the panel of stone-faced officers whether I inhaled or not. Maybe I had a small chance. Now just like going on an operation or setting up for an ambush, I had to focus and to push whatever I was feeling down deep, or I was going to lose my freedom.

Captain Williams looked as nervous as I felt when he looked up from his notes and walked around in front of his desk, facing me as I stood at the edge of the table. His voice sounded like he hadn't inhaled quite enough air when he asked me to describe the events that happened on 12 September, starting with what I was in the hospital for and the events from there on.

I told the story in detail without stopping, from the insect bite in Mexico to where the CID agents searched my car and wall and footlockers. No one asked me any questions. I looked over at Williams a couple of times; he just appeared to subtly shrug his shoulders and raise his eyebrows like "just keep on going." It seemed like with every breath and every word I was unwinding a little more.

It was a real blessing to my defense that Jasper had been in the accident, proving that he was indeed in possession of my car during the weekend, and I hadn't hesitated to sign statements that allowed the CID agents to search my car.

By the time I reached the story where the CID agents turned us over to our company commander, Williams and I were both more much more relaxed. Williams walked around to the front of his desk, pacing slowly back and forth, asking me several quick questions to help establish my innocence—sort of Perry Mason–style. "Did you take a puff off the marijuana cigarette down by the Lake with Lance Corporal Jasper and Ing?" "Did you know that there was marijuana in the glove compartment of my car?" I remembered to look at the panel of judges as I answered each in a calm voice: "No, sir."

Williams looked down at his notes and then asked me if I knew if Lance Corporal Jasper used marijuana prior to this incident. I responded: "Lance Corporal Jasper was apprehended for possession of marijuana in San Diego, the same time I was working in the company office writing the unit diary, so I wrote up the entire incident when I submitted the diary to headquarters."

Williams then asked me why I suspected the cigarette Jasper was smoking down by the lake was marijuana. I replied, "I had smelled it before in Vietnam."

Williams checked his notes and asked me to explain to the court how the CID agents found a book of Zig-Zag rolling papers and one charred seed when I was first asked me to empty my robe pockets. My immediate response was that when I saw the post mistress approaching us, I grabbed the joint from Private Ing's hand, and while stubbing it out I saw the book of rolling papers on the ground and put them both in my robe pocket. When asked to empty my pockets at headquarters I pulled out my wallet and the seed and papers fell out onto the table.

All the trial officers looked up when Williams asked me to show the court my folding type of wallet, which I did. He then checked his notes and in a louder voice said, "No further questions."

Captain John D. Moats USMC, the trial counsel for the government, stood and came from behind his table to face me. He was a broad-shouldered squared-away marine with an impressive set of ribbons on his chest. It seemed to me that Moats felt that this court-martial was just a whole bunch of hogwash and that he would just as soon declare I was not guilty and person-ally escort me out to the parking lot.

He asked me no more than half a dozen questions, for example: "How many times while you were in country had you smelled marijuana, where had you smelled it, and how long had you been back from Vietnam." Moats then took a quarter turn to face the panel of officers and said, "I don't have any more questions."

What? That's it for the government's council? For about a split second, before I could even feel a fleeting touch of exhilaration, that maybe this was it, that I was finished testifying.

Colonel William W. Wander, like a drill instructor, barked out, "I have."

I think my heart skipped a beat when I looked in the face of Wander. His weathered, deeply lined face, bushy eyebrows, and white hair gave him the appearance of a rugged Marine Corps officer.

Wander asked to know how well I knew Lance Corporal Jasper and if I was aware he was smoking marijuana aboard base. I stated that I knew Jasper for only about three months. Wander asked why I lent my brown corduroy sport jacket to someone I didn't know very well, to which I replied the jacket didn't mean all that much to me, and I didn't want to lug it home on leave.

For a long ten seconds Wander just looked at me like maybe he had forgotten his next question. He hadn't. Seemingly out of the blue, Wander asked: "Did you smoke marijuana in Vietnam?" Without hesitation, I replied: "Yes, sir, I did."

Williams's head snapped up from viewing the paperwork on his desk so fast that he dislodged his glasses; I was looking right at him. Whatever my panel of judges had been thinking up to this moment, vanished. Wander had thrown the big punch, and it connected.

Wander squinted at me as if he were taking aim. He cleared his throat and took a breath, like he wanted all of this to soak in. In a relatively quiet voice Wander asked, "About how many times did you smoke it?"

"Approximately twice, sir."

"That's all you smoked it, was twice?" His voice definitely had gone up a couple of clicks.

"Yes, sir. The first time, I didn't like the effect that gave me. It was after a mortar attack, and we were in a bunker. Several people were passing a joint around, and when it came to me, the marine sitting next to me said, 'Go ahead and try it, it ain't going to kill ya.' And at the time I—I—I was real fatalistic; I still had a long time in country to go. I tried it, and it just gave me a headache. The second time was about two months later to similar circumstances. It made me lightheaded, and I couldn't judge myself. I couldn't function like the way I wanted to, it just wasn't for me."

"Where were you in Vietnam when that happened?" Wander, not taking his eyes off of me, injected into my pause.

"That happened at Camp Carroll, sir."

"Where is that? Northern Vietnam?"

About that time, to use an old cliché, you really could have heard a pin drop in the court room. I was not going to correct the colonel on his geography; we were still in South Vietnam, next to the DMZ. "Yes, sir, it is. Right up on the edge. It's well—it's about six miles North from Cam Lo."

"What about the second time you used it?"

"That's where I tried it a second time."

"At the same spot?" The colonel finally broke eye contact with me to look at the papers in front of him.

"Yes, sir."

"What were your duties at that time?" Wander shifted his eyes back to mine.

"I was a Third Marine regimental scout/sniper, sir."

"All right." Wander glanced down to his notes. "You smoked on two different occasions? How much did you smoke on each occasion?"

"Well, the first time I just—I just stayed in the bunker with them. There were about three or four people, and they were just passing one around. On the second time, there were three people—that's including myself—and we smoked two of them."

"So," queried the colonel, "the first time, did you yourself smoke one whole joint—ah, one whole cigarette?"

"No, not a full one," I said. "They were just passed around a bunch of people."

"Can you tell us approximately how many puffs or draws or drags you had on it?" Wander nodded to the officers seated next to him.

I took a deep breath before responding: "Maybe four or five—four—four or five."

"Okay, what about a second time? There were three of you who smoked two cigarettes. Is that correct?"

"That's right."

"Would you say you consumed one cigarette at that time?" A badgering or cynical tone entered his voice.

"I think I consumed just about two thirds of one cigarette or close to it." *This guy is coming after me, and I had better get my guard up.*

Wander glanced down, then looked up from his papers and squinted at me like he was drawing a bead, and began several rapid-fire questions: "Have you smoked marijuana at any other time?"

"No, sir, I haven't."

"How about before you came into the Marine Corps?" His voice was getting a little louder.

"No, sir."

"Have you smoked any since you got back?"

"No, sir, I haven't." Lying under oath was giving me a sinking feeling.

A pause. Wander stared briefly off to the back of the room. Then, eyes back to mine, he stated: "Got one more question."

Wander again took a few extra-long seconds, glancing down, then looked up from his papers, "Are you aware of the regulations aboard this base about personnel other than yourself smoking marijuana? Say perhaps, if you were perhaps, aware of what they were smoking—" His voice and question kind of drifted off.

"Well," I said with not as much certainty, "up to this occurrence I wasn't sure of the penalties, but I knew the penalties were very stiff."

"I'm not talking about the penalties, now!" Wander blurted out, obviously irritated: "Did you know at the time, when you had an idea that Jasper was smoking, did you know your responsibilities in regard to report this man?"

"Yes." I took a pause. I didn't like where this was going. "Yes, I did."

"Did you make any report?" Wander now raised his voice in an accusatory tone. "I'm not talking about specifically the time that you were apprehended. I'm talking about any previous instances."

I felt then Colonel Wander had me by the short hairs. "Well," I responded with what I thought was a calm voice, "the reason I gave him back the marijuana cigarette, after I took it from him, is that while I was in Vietnam, I observe numerous people who I knew, smoked, and to me I thought that one has to make their own mind up about it, and I had already made up my mind. I knew he was in the wrong, but he seemed like an incorrigible because he was caught before, and he was getting out soon."

"Once again, are you referring to the time down by the lake?" Wander glaring at me, now visibly exasperated.

"Yes, I am."

"I'm talking about any previous instances. Anytime that you might have had suspicions that he or anybody else was smoking marijuana prior to that date?" Wander's tone now caused the other officers to look at him.

"Oh, I see." I had to come up with something quick. "No, I didn't have any report then, I did, at one time, while I was holding inspections and it—it was in the formation, and I inspected, my squad—he had extremely bloodshot eyes and I mentioned it to the platoon sergeant."

"Did you give the platoon sergeant any reason to believe—any reason whatsoever?"

"I just said that Jasper looks like he's pretty—well, drunk. Now, whether it was alcohol—I couldn't smell any alcohol, but that was after he'd come back to the company—after he had finished his time in jail."

Wander, silent, shuffled his papers momentarily: "I have nothing further."

I think Captain Williams was highly pissed that I admitted to smoking marijuana in Vietnam. It almost seemed like he tried to sink the boat with his closing questions.

"Would you just state your, your position on marijuana? Did you enjoy using it?" he almost hissed.

"No, I didn't," I said, a little taken back by the question and its tone. How was answering this going to help me? "I don't drink alcohol for the same reason. I don't like the feeling of not being able to control my actions."

In the same accusing voice he said, "Would you use it again if it was offered to you?"

"No, I wouldn't. I made up my mind about it, and that's all there is to it."

"As to how soon, did you have suspicions—did you have that Jasper was using marijuana prior to actually being down at the—Lake O'Neil?"

What? What kind of question was that? Did he miss the whole part about the unit diary and Jasper being arrested for marijuana in San Diego?

"Not that strong," I answered, "because I wasn't around him that much. It was just on several occasions I . . . I noticed his eyes were extra bloodshot or he . . . he just would come up and start talking to me about something—just off-the-wall stuff."

"No further questions."

At this point I was feeling numb. As I made it to my seat, Lieutenant Clark, my platoon commander while I was a squad leader in the grunts, was called to the stand to testify as to my character. Clark was a hard-core marine with a thick neck and barrel chest. Although we never talked about it in depth, I know he'd seen plenty of action. He had been back in the states for about six months. I had a lot of respect for the lieutenant as our platoon commander, especially how he worked when we were in the field with a bunch of seventen-year-old privates. I'm sure he volunteered to come down and testify. That's the kind of person he was.

"State your full name, rank, organization, and armed force, please."

"Stephen Patrick Clark, First Lieutenant United States Marine Corps, Foxtrot, Second Battalion, 28th Marines, weapons platoon commander."

The lieutenant seemed kind of nervous.

My defense council, Williams, also looked nervous now, and it made me feel nervous. His first big trial or not, this was years of my life on the line. He looked from his papers toward Clark and asked, "Are you acquainted with the accused in this case?"

"Yes, I am."

"Could you state his name and point to him?" Williams turned toward me as Clark pointed at me.

Wander noted, "Let the record show that the witness pointed to the accused present."

Williams then asked, "Lieutenant Clark, would you please tell us how well you know the accused?"

Clark's eyes darted around the courtroom as he said, "Do I speak to the Captain or the court or . . . ?"

"Just make sure the reporter hears you," prompted Wander.

"I became platoon commander about the last week in August and have been the platoon commander since that time."

Williams slowly paced in front of his table while he asked, "What is your opinion of Corporal Nutting as to his truth?"

"Well, I believe the reason I'm down here at all is—is I have a very high opinion of him. I have every reason to believe him. He's been trusted on several occasions with jobs to do for me, and for the platoon, assumed the jobs of . . . initially done by higher-ranking NCOs requiring supervision, without someone of higher rank being around. I have never had any question or doubt. He's done a very good job the whole time he's been there."

"Have you had occasion to mark Corporal Nutting since you have taken over the platoon?"

"No, I have not," Clark responded.

"If you were to mark him on say a five-point scale," asked Williams, "where would you put him?"

"You mean . . . ?"

"As far as conduct and proficiency marks are concerned."

"I would probably mark four point six for proficiency, and four point seven for conduct," Clark replied without hesitation.

"Are you aware that Corporal Nutting has smoked marijuana two times while he was in Vietnam?"

"No, I was not."

"Given that knowledge—that he has smoked marijuana on two different occasions," Williams questioned, "let us assume that he was being recommended for an administrative discharge based on that use. Would you recommend retaining him with the Marine Corps or recommend that he be administratively discharged?"

"Just based on what you said, I don't think I could use—the only thing I could use relative to that is my experience with him—my observation of him. That is to say, even though I am firmly against marijuana any time or place, I believe a severe penalty should be involved with it . . . the performance I have observed . . . I have never seen his work impaired at all. I think he's a credit to the Marine Corps and I have to say. . . that keep him in unless some previous conviction or something would be under present policy to force him to be considered for discharge."

Williams reiterated, "Have you ever had any reason at all to suspect that Corporal Nutting was using marijuana while here in the United States?"

"The only way I could ever get information on that," Clark replied, "would be personal observation, poor performance, or maybe just my opinion of what he looked like or, sometimes if he had been drinking or not, or hearsay and I've never had either one—either type of information." All the while, Clark was giving me an "I did the best I could" kind of look.

"Thank you. I don't have any more questions."

I have no clear memory of when the court adjourned, except having that old sick feeling of being in someone's crosshairs as the officers who held my future filed out of the courtroom.

35

I tried to avoid eye contact as Delgado and I made our way out of the judicial building through the side door leading to the parking lots. The little alcove we visited earlier in the day had grown an inviting sliver of shade.

I lit a cigarette and tried to calm a growing feeling of desperation. My mind was flooded with a jumble of thoughts. The court-martial, my family, my friends killed in Vietnam—I could not stop my mind from racing.

Between the court being adjourned and the verdict my thoughts reflected back to a conversation with the unit diary clerk who had taken my place in the company office. He told me then that Rodrigues made several changes in my service record book. Rodrigues, according to the new diary clerk, changed my proficiency and my conduct marks to 4.1 and 4.1 from 4.6 to 4.8, respectively. Furthermore, my service record book, at the time of the trial, shows I barely qualify as a marksman instead of an expert. The only way a marine with an MOS of 0351 anti-assault man could serve as a regimental scout/sniper is with an expert qualification out of boot camp.

When I absolutely had to have a conversation with him, he seemed almost apoplectic. His pseudo-smile had a grimace quality, and his eyes had a little extra crazy in them. It was well-known throughout the company office that Rodrigues had his heart set on me spending hard time in Leavenworth for the next seven to ten years. At the moment sitting out there in the sunshine with Lance Corporal Delgado waiting for my verdict to come in, thinking about Rodrigues just added to my sinking feeling of desperation.

An ugly growing sense of panic, of being trapped, with no way out, made me feel like I couldn't get enough air.

I had to get control of myself. I had to start thinking positive thoughts or I could have a meltdown. My mind drifted to gentle, sweet, soft-spoken Katherine, who could be waiting for me right now, in a parking lot just outside the main gate. She vowed to wait all day and into the night, if necessary.

Katherine spent many hours over the past months trying to convince me how easy it would be to go to the East Coast with her and disappear into one of the many communes starting up around the country.

Our last weekend together was tumultuous, to say the least. Passionate lovemaking interspersed with Katherine tearfully pleading with me to run away with her. Katherine's older brother was an activist in the peace movement to end the Vietnam war. As she put it, he thought he was a "hot shit lawyer," but he did have "some very solid connections." He had helped other people who didn't want to go to Vietnam. According to Katherine, her brother could get me every kind of identification I needed. I could become a completely different person and start a new life. I don't think I ever considered any of her propositions seriously at the time, but I very much enjoyed her tender attempts at convincing me.

I didn't want to start a new life, and I didn't want to run away from my old one.

I told Delgado I needed to walk or I was going to go bug fuck. Delgado said it was okay with him as long as we stayed in the general parking lot area. We walked to the end of the sidewalk at the edge of the parking lot and turned around when I spotted a station wagon. The driver was a woman appearing to be looking for a parking space. In the station wagon with her were two children. The girl in the back seat was an early teenager; the boy in the passenger seat was probably nine or ten years old. The boy and I made eye contact for a good ten seconds, until his mom turned down a row of parked cars. He looked all spiffed up, with a freshly butch waxed crew cut and a madras sport shirt. I felt at the time he was coming to see or pick up his father.

Increasingly in the months leading up to my court-martial, the many dead faces and how they looked when I last saw them became almost like a waking mantra that I couldn't shut off. There were times when alone I would talk to them.

I prayed for God to give me strength.

Walking with Delgado to the end of the sidewalk, I had what only could be described as a moment of clarity. Isn't that what we all wanted, what we all talked about more or less, down in the bunker? I could almost hear them and see their faces. If only we were lucky enough to live through this hellish place, we would go school on the GI Bill, buy a car, find the girl of our dreams, get a place of our own, maybe raise a family, and live the rest our lives in peace.

I just had to get through this. I had to go and live the life we all had hoped for when we were just voices talking of home in the pitch-dark security of a sandbagged bunker. Delgado and I turned around where the parking lot began and started back to the judicial building.

Epilogue

It had taken the officers of the court a little over three hours to reach a verdict. I remember standing at rigid attention while the judges filed back into their seats and the court reconvened.

I was standing at attention with my knees slightly buckled, when the law officer, Colonel William W. Wander, finally broke the long silence. Even after almost forty years, the memory of this moment is as vivid in my memory as the day it happened.

"Not guilty of all charges and specifications."

The court adjourned at 1548 hours, 24 March 1969.

Afterword

Like I said at the very beginning of this story, the main reason for writing this account is for my children, or who comes after, if they want to know what happened to me, from my words, during this tumultuous period in our history.

Sometimes, it was plain procrastination for not writing; other times, it felt too painful to remember and write about. I have always wondered how I would end this story. I enjoyed reading the trial transcription. Although I knew the outcome, I discovered I'd forgotten some details.

Opening Pandora's box, and reading and thinking about an incident I buried long ago, I found I still have that old guilty feeling for lying under oath. The other side of the coin is: What if? What if I had fessed up and told it exactly how it happened? If I had been found guilty and spent years in a federal prison, my life, my family, and the lives of those people around me would have been profoundly different. I remembered only a few things from the end of the trial until the time I was separated from the Marine Corps with an honorable discharge two weeks later. Katherine flew back to the East Coast the morning of my trial. I think she sort of cracked under the pressure of me getting ready for this court-martial after the other two postponements. She called me a month later in Idaho, remorseful and tearful, wanting me to fly to Boston to be with her. I told her I'd think about it. I never called her back.

I bumped into Sergeant Rodrigues several times after the court-martial and before discharge. I had seen my Service Record Book many times while I worked in the company office. My proficiency and conduct marks ranged from 4.6 to 4.8, respectively. There is no proof, but I do know that it would have been very easy for Rodrigues to make the changes. I remember him as an uptight asshole, and it is interesting for me to see, after all these years, the lengths he probably went to seek his petty revenge.

I will end this story, my dear reader, with one of my most vivid memories of that time. I remember very little about being discharged from the Marine Corps earlier that day. What I do remember clearly, almost like it happened last week, was this: I was driving home on the I-5 freeway in my faithful Ford Fairlane, with her newly acquired flower power decals. I made it! I was out. I couldn't believe it; I was going home. I was going to get a life after Vietnam. I was thinking about how many times the bullets snapped over my head or when I was "just in that spot, a minute ago." How did I survive that? Am I really going home? How was it, that as long as I was in Vietnam, and as long as I was a sniper, I never put the crosshairs on someone and pulled the trigger? I shot white phosphorous rockets at the enemy bunkers to mark them. I fired at muzzle flashes in the dark. I laid down covering fire in ambushes. I spotted the enemy and called in shots working in a sniper team. But as hard as I tried, I never looked at the face of a dead enemy and knew for certain that it was me who pulled the trigger. How could that happen?

The loud car radio didn't drown out the thoughts that filled my head that day as I smoked cigarettes with the window rolled down. I have a profound memory of the intense feeling I had inside. It's the same feeling from when you were a little kid, and there was something in the dark and you weren't sure what it was, but it was right behind you. It was the same feeling in Vietnam, while I was on a night ambush or staring out into the pitch black for hours on some remote listening post. I had that same feeling while I was driving away from Camp Pendleton; I had ducked a major bullet that almost cost me years of my life, and now I had to get away. As each mile turned on the odometer, I felt a little better inside. I had made it, and now I was going home!

I had driven a little over an hour a when I glanced out the driver's-side window. Although it was just about a second (this image is still burned in my brain), I saw a young man, maybe in his midtwenties, flying through the air about ten feet away from me with his dirt-covered face in my direction. He was in the fetal position. His eyes were squinted shut. I looked in my rearview mirror and saw a large cloud of dust rising up behind me. I don't remember any car flying through the air or seeing the victim hitting the ground. But I do remember how I felt; there it is again, another close call, a matter of seconds, and just a few inches. How close was I to the car accident I never saw coming or happen? That "it" out there had almost gotten me again. It had been right behind me, had been closing in, and just missed me.

* * *

Writing about Art Vigil's and Tom Burkhardt's deaths was particularly tough. It was painful to remember and write about. I wanted to keep this as accurate as I possibly could, but I could not remember the day they were killed. I looked through my notes and letters and finally after several days, I had a Luddite's eureka moment; I could go online and find their names on the Vietnam Veterans Memorial Wall site. At the site, under Art's name was a bar that said "personal comments or pictures click here" so I clicked on it. At the site were several paragraphs written by Art's little brother Duane, who said that soon he would be a grandfather and that one of the things that saddened him in his life was that his children never knew what a really cool big brother he had. Several weeks went by, and I thought about it every day. Finally, I sent an e-mail to Duane, saying that that I knew Art and had loved him like a brother and that I was with him the day he died. He immediately responded with questions like: What happened? Did he suffer? Why was he on that patrol anyway? Questions about all the things that I had just written about. We wrote back and forth several times. He told me that their mother is still alive in her nineties and still grieves Art's death. I struggled with the idea of sending chapter 15 to him. It was a hard chapter for me to write, and it was still in very rough form. Finally, I wrote to him saying there is wisdom in the old saying, "Ignorance is bliss," and maybe it was best to remember Arthur how he was and that he came home from Vietnam in a coffin. I told Duane that although it was still very rough, I would send him everything that I'd written about Art. I cautioned him that anyone who knew and loved Arthur, would probably want to go someplace quiet and by themselves. Sometime later I received an e-mail from Duane, saying that he and his brother (I didn't know Art had two brothers), decided not to show their mom what I had written. Duane said his little brother took it particularly hard. In his last e-mail, Duane told me of his memories of Art as his big brother and the kind of guy he was in high school. He said that the family was very grateful for the information, and that after all these years of putting it off, going to the Vietnam Wall was in their plans for the near future.